Detection Avoidance in Homicides

Detection Avoidance in Homicides: Debates, Explanations and Responses presents theory and research on how offenders avoid detection and the challenges and opportunities these efforts pose to investigators.

From a scholarly perspective, the book presents a continuing history of research on detection avoidance by offenders, discusses the features of complex death investigations involving detection avoidance and critiques the current frameworks used for conceptualizing these behaviors. Dr. Ferguson focuses on the key debates in the literature, argues for collaborations between researchers and practitioners to remedy siloing and explores the reality of detection avoidance in homicides as complex and multifaceted. While detection avoidance behaviors have the potential to negatively impact sudden death investigations and frustrate criminal investigations specifically, their use also creates broader problems. These include many problematic effects on family members of the deceased, police officers, police agencies and the communities they serve. Offenders choosing to use detection avoidance behaviors challenge the efficient use of public resources, put at risk the successful adjudication of homicides and create a public safety issue. The book explains detection avoidance using learning, situational, individual and gender-based theories, including proposing whether it may be a form of coercive control used by intimate partner abusers. Finally, how detection avoidance by offenders is recognized and responded to in sudden death investigations is addressed, with specific reference to useful examples of policy reform implemented by various police agencies internationally.

Providing research and theory to explain detection avoidance and best practice for responding to it, this book will be of great interest to students and scholars of criminology, forensic science and psychology. It will also be useful to professionals working with homicide offenders.

Claire Ferguson is a Senior Lecturer and researcher in the School of Justice at Queensland University of Technology in Brisbane, Australia. Claire's work bridges the gap between theory and practice in complex sudden death investigations potentially involving detection avoidance. While she has published over 40 articles in many academic journals, she also uses her research to inform training and expert consultancy for assisting police, attorneys and coroners investigating missing persons, equivocal deaths and suspected homicides.

Routledge Studies in Criminal Behaviour

The Psychology of Crime, Policing and Courts
Edited by Andreas Kapardis and David P. Farrington

The Sexual Murderer
Offender behaviour and implications for practice
Eric Beauregard and Melissa Martineau

Psychological Violence in the Workplace
New perspectives and shifting frameworks
Emily Schindeler, Janet Ransley and Danielle Reynald

Domestic Homicide
Patterns and Dynamics
Marieke Liem and Frans Koenraadt

Intergenerational Continuity of Criminal and Antisocial Behaviour
An International Overview of Studies
Edited by Veroni I. Eichelsheim and Steve G. A. van de Weijer

Evidence-Based Offender Profiling
Edited by Bryanna H. Fox, David P. Farrington, Andreas Kapardis and Olivia C. Hambly

Empathy versus Offending, Aggression and Bullying
Advancing Knowledge using the Basic Empathy Scale
Darrick Jolliffe and David P. Farrington

For more information about this series, please visit: https://www.routledge.com/Routledge-Studies-in-Criminal-Behaviour/book-series/RSCB

Detection Avoidance in Homicides

Debates, Explanations and Responses

Claire Ferguson

Routledge
Taylor & Francis Group
LONDON AND NEW YORK

First published 2021
by Routledge
2 Park Square, Milton Park, Abingdon, Oxon OX14 4RN

and by Routledge
52 Vanderbilt Avenue, New York, NY 10017

Routledge is an imprint of the Taylor & Francis Group, an informa business

British Library Cataloguing-in-Publication Data
A catalogue record for this book is available from the British Library

Library of Congress Cataloging-in-Publication Data
A catalog record has been requested for this book

ISBN: 9780367266875 (hbk)
ISBN: 9780367521387 (pbk)
ISBN: 9780367266851 (ebk)

Typeset in Times New Roman
by codeMantra

Contents

Preface

Common sense tells us that any reasoning murderer is likely to try to avoid being detected for their crime. In perfect circumstances, offenders might use any number of detection avoidance (DA) behaviors to do so, including lying to police, preventing evidence being deposited at the death scene, destroying evidence tying them to scene or victim and/or concealing the homicide. However, the reality borne out of the research is that many homicide offenders do not seem to use any countermeasures at all. This is despite the real and perceived benefits such behaviors can provide to offenders.

Failing to use DA might be due to the fact that for many offenders, their homicides are impulsive and they simply do not think of DA in the moment. It may be that some offenders experience a fight or flight response after committing a homicide, and they therefore flee the scene before being able to use DA. Or, it may be that some offenders do not believe they will be suspected or tied to the homicide in the first place, meaning that DA is not required. Given the state of literature on DA at the moment, we cannot say for sure which of these factors, if any, is influencing the decision-making of any offender at any time. Perhaps more importantly, we also cannot say for sure why certain offenders and/or types of offenders *do* use countermeasures during the commission of a homicide. Very few theories have been tested to help explain when, why and how DA behaviors are used during the commission of homicides.

If many, maybe even most, homicide offenders do not use any form of DA behavior in committing their crime, why should we spend time and resources attempting to describe and explain DA when it is present? Given the very limited resources available for death and homicide investigations in police agencies and the push toward preventing volume crime with more wide-ranging implications, this is a question which cannot be taken for granted. There are several major reasons why studying DA is necessary, though some would argue that any one of these alone is enough.

First, there is strong evidence to suggest that the use of DA behaviors can have a real impact on homicides being correctly classified as suspicious and criminal deaths, and then properly investigated as such. As will be discussed throughout this book, there are numerous examples of cases that have been wrongly classified as non-suspicious deaths based on the DA behaviors of offenders, and other examples of homicides that are correctly classified but remain unsolved due to a lack of evidence from DA. We know about many misclassified cases due to continuing investigations by journalists and the media, usually after many pleas from the decedent's family to the responsible police agency. These unofficial investigations may uncover worrying evidence of homicide and cause officials to reopen the case. They can also have problematic outcomes for the corresponding agencies as a result, including a reduction in confidence held by the public.

Other misclassified homicides are eventually discovered due to new information coming into the hands of police who are open to hearing it and able to understand its significance, and in agencies that have time and resources to devote to reinvestigating closed cases. The upshot of uncovering these concealed homicides after some period of time, and hopefully solving them, is the uncomfortable associated question – how many more of these cases are there? The sheer number of examples of misclassified, unclassified and unsolved homicides involving DA indicates that there may be many we have yet to identify, meaning that there could be a significant number of offenders who have literally gotten away with murder. Understanding DA behavior, and thus being able to identify it, is necessary to prevent cases being misclassified or remaining unsolved, therefore also preventing all issues failing to recognize these behaviors creates, including impacts on families, police themselves and public confidence.

The second reason DA in homicide warrants attention is that a failure to understand DA in both police and criminology circles significantly affects the welfare of families dealing with the sudden death of a loved one and their corresponding confidence in the police investigation. Experiencing the sudden death of a family member is likely to be the worst thing that happens to someone in their lifetime. Adding to that, a feeling of uncertainty surrounding whether the death was properly investigated, whether the family truly knows what happened to their loved one and whether a responsible person has not been held to account only makes the difficulty of such a situation more pronounced for family members. In cases where homicides are wrongly classified for a period of time, families commonly report devoting their life to seeking justice for their loved one. Being overruled or not listened to by police creates a sense of injustice that is profound, life altering and unlikely to be understood by anyone who has not experienced it. Putting aside the motivation to properly and efficiently investigate possible homicides, a desire to avoid these negative impacts on family members alone is enough to warrant further study, understanding and training surrounding DA and homicide.

In a similar vein, the available research indicates that police officers themselves experience significant frustration in carrying out complex death investigations possibly involving DA. This is especially true in cases involving fatal falls, hanging deaths and long-term missing people. In doing this research and training police, it is not uncommon for them to share (usually off the record) that they always suspected later-uncovered homicides were not being given the attention and resourcing that they deserved. These detectives report feeling paralyzed by an inability to attain necessary resources because they could not demonstrate unequivocally that the death was a homicide. Failing to satisfy the powers that be that a homicide has occurred leads to resources of all types being drastically limited, including the time officers are afforded to further investigate, the forensic testing an agency will commit to or pay for and the use of outside expertise to assist.

In missing persons cases where an offender has disposed of the victim's body as a form of DA, investigators have even reported that these difficult cases are the beginning of the end of their careers in policing. So frustrated are investigators with looking for a person they suspect to have been murdered and not receiving the support and resources they feel they need that they end up fatigued, disheartened and ultimately leave the police service. Such a loss of investigative experience and commitment to victims sends immeasurable ripple effects through police agencies, police officers, their families and victims' families. Far-reaching implications such as these again speak to the necessity of better understanding and identifying DA and developing best practice to adequately resource cases where DA appears or is suspected. Ultimately, even if DA happens in the minority of homicide cases, we need to do better for the officers it impacts so that they can identify and adequately investigate such cases, thus better serving the families involved and the community they work for.

Finally, there is also strong evidence suggesting that our failure to understand DA has an impact on practical aspects of investigating and prosecuting homicide offenders who use DA to their advantage. A lack of research on DA creates significant problems with locating experts who can testify in court about whether DA is indeed present in a given case. Expert testimony being admitted requires a sound theoretical and empirical basis in most jurisdictions using a common law system. Unfortunately, the absence of robust empirical literature and theorizing surrounding DA means that the majority of homicide experts may not be able to meet the thresholds of the court when it comes to expertise surrounding DA. Therefore, judges and juries may miss out on the opportunity to learn from experts what we know about DA and whether it is likely to have occurred in the case at hand. Of course, this has implications for successfully prosecuting offenders and precluding further effects of their DA behavior.

The lack of research also impacts on how efficiently limited police resources can be used in sudden death investigations where DA might be present. A failure to systematically examine DA in the homicide research means that each policing agency faced with a difficult case is on their own in terms of using resources effectively. There is currently no best practice for uncovering DA in homicides, nor progressing with investigations once DA is discovered. The inefficiency associated with each agency having to reinvent the wheel in problematic cases, where resources are often very limited to begin with, makes a strong argument for better understanding DA through good research, theorizing and collaboration between researchers and police.

So, more needs to be known about DA in homicides, both from a theoretical and practical perspective, and for a number of reasons. Along with indicating when and how DA is perpetrated in homicides, the first questions that need to be answered surround key debates regarding definitions of DA, as well as proposing theoretical explanations for these behaviors and possible responses. Both the process and result of answering these questions will help to get investigators and academics on the same page, informing both empirical and forensic analyses of behaviors that have not been observed previously. One of the main things that needs to happen to inform this area, and indeed a major aim of this book, is to encourage communication and collaboration between academics and practitioners. Such cooperative relationships to remove the evident silos are necessary between medical and policing practitioners when it comes to making manner of death determinations as well, an issue which is discussed in the chapters to follow.

Both theoretical and practice-specific development is also necessary when it comes to unpacking links between DA and intimate partner violence (IPV)/intimate partner homicide (IPH) specifically. This area has received some attention in recent years, especially when it comes to concealed homicides, but robust research and theorizing is overdue. It is hoped that this book will go some way to further exploring and explaining why intimate partner abusers are drawn to DA behaviors and how investigators might be trained to recognize and respond to DA in the perpetration of IPH.

Finally, it is clear that work needs to be done to empower detectives to be able to do their jobs to the best of their ability. As will become clear in the following pages, homicides involving DA are most often solved by good old-fashioned police work. This requires education and training in these skills, adequate resources being made available to detectives responsible for sudden death investigations and support from policing agencies at various levels of the hierarchy. It is hoped that this book will contribute to the argument for better policy, training and investigative aids that will foster these skills and support the careers of the next generation of good detectives. They have an incredibly difficult job to do when it comes to sudden death investigations and we need them to feel reassured in their ability to do exemplary work.

To meet the ambitious aims of this book, Chapter 1 will first outline some of the key discussions of DA in homicide in the early criminology and forensic science literature. Despite many of these being written over 50 years ago, the lessons described in these texts are still timely. This is especially true when it comes to the necessity for effective cooperation between police and researchers. While summarizing the early and then contemporary works on DA, the major debates in the literature will also be explored, including issues with defining DA and crime scene staging (CSS) that continue to create problems in this area, even decades after the behaviors were first identified.

Chapter 2 explores the basics of DA in homicides, including rates of DA use by offenders, behaviors commonly employed and crime types where DA is most likely to be present. The importance of studying victim and offender relationships are explored in this chapter, introducing the apparent attraction that intimate partner murderers feel toward the use of DA. Along with outlining common DA behaviors, notable effects of these on the solvability of homicide are also proposed, including a possible framework for their impact on investigations.

In Chapter 3, the academic literature attempting to categorize DA in homicides is explored. Three significant efforts to classify and explain DA and CSS are reviewed and issues with the usefulness and validity of each typology are explored. The overarching theme of this chapter is that, although DA behaviors in homicide appear to be quite simply teased apart and easily studied, in fact the reality of the use of DA by offenders appears much more complex.

Chapter 4 likens DA and CSS to deception more broadly and explores whether the robust literature on deception detection may therefore be useful for uncovering DA. In so doing, it argues that training investigators to detect lies in suspect interviews may not be the most useful way forward for recognizing DA in sudden death investigations.

The theories that have been proposed to explain DA are outlined in Chapter 5. Learning, situational and individual theories are used to position DA offenders as rational, manipulative and sometimes well prepared. In so doing, links between DA and psychopathy are drawn, both empirically and intuitively, showing that choosing to use DA may be a function of multiple factors at various levels.

Chapter 6 describes DA as a possible form of coercive control, commonly seen in IPV and intimate partner femicide (IPF) cases. Using case examples, it argues that reasoning offenders with an intimate knowledge of their victims are attracted to using DA during commission of a homicide as doing so provides opportunities for more than just avoiding detection. Using and threatening to use DA allows offenders to control their victims in life and death, and therefore may appeal to perpetrators for several reasons.

Finally, Chapter 7 addresses the question – what can we do to respond to DA by offenders and prevent the negative effects of these behaviors? The challenges facing detectives investigating sudden deaths are first outlined. Then, the academic research and example policing responses are used to argue for evidence-based policy reform, including implementing training, enhancing supervision requirements and changes to procedure in the form of investigative aids.

Together, these chapters demonstrate that much work still needs to be done to better identify, explain and respond to DA by offenders during the commission of homicides. This book argues that through effective collaboration between academics and police, the key debates that have limited this area of research and practice can be resolved. This book shows that even with these limitations and even though progress has been siloed, significant strides have been made toward preventing the DA behavior of offenders from negatively affecting sudden death investigations. It is hoped that the momentum achieved by academics and investigators alike, described within these pages, will continue to evolve into the future so that victims, families, detectives, police agencies and the public can win out over offenders attempting to avoid detection.

Acknowledgments

I am so grateful for the opportunity to acknowledge all the wonderful, patient and helpful people who have assisted me with writing this book. Before I do so though, a bit of context on how the project progressed is required. I hope you will bear with me.

I began planning this book at the end of 2019. At that point, I had recently finished a productive sabbatical and I was full of ideas. Going back to work at the beginning of 2020, I was inundated with teaching and administrative tasks. All I wanted to do was get my ideas on paper before I forgot them. I made notes (which were later indecipherable) in the moments between meetings and lectures. I scheduled my year with plenty of writing planned in the supposed "quiet time" between grant season, marking and some work with police agencies. I was confident it would all come together by the end of the year.

And then a global pandemic hit.

Needless to say, the writing schedule changed rapidly and dramatically. There was not going to be any quiet time this year. The "good ideas" would have to be developed when I wasn't making arrangements to move everything online and into a remote set up. I would have to be very efficient – admittedly not something academics are known for – to get all the ideas on paper in a way that was presentable to the world. I had my work cut out for me, but I optimistically figured the sense of urgency might help with staying motivated. Then the universe delivered two things that took me from optimistic to frantic: in May I got pregnant and in June I lost all the data on my computer, which had, rather inconveniently, not been backed up since January.[1]

Right. I did not want my good ideas to go to waste, but writing this book was becoming *a bit* stressful. I decided I needed an attitude change. My existing efficiency morphed into ruthless productivity; the ideas were quickly streamlined into those which absolutely needed to be discussed. I became very focused in my critique of the research, thinking only pragmatically about how we view and discuss the issue of DA in both the academic and policing communities. The pressure of writing this book in the context of my life in 2020 forced me to step back and look for the overarching issues preventing us all from being better able to explain and respond to DA in homicides.

The result of this pragmatism is a book that, I hope, will help bridge the gap between those trying to resolve difficult death cases every day and those attempting to research and explain the behaviors of offenders perpetrating homicides and DA. I hope that the book, though covering a wide range of topics relevant to theory and practice, will assist both investigators and academics in their individual and collaborative work. Such assistance for everyone struggling to understand DA at death scenes is timely and deserved.

Although writing a book in 2020 was difficult, thankfully I was not alone in my efforts. I was inspired and pushed forward by reviewing the work of many of my previous coauthors, including Dr. Wayne Petherick, Dr. Kamarah Pooley and Ms. Tiffany Sutherland. Thank you for working with me on the projects we did together and for bringing such fresh perspectives to them. Your input has helped me immensely and shaped the direction of this book.

Dr. Laura Pettler and her work on crime scene staging also spurred me along this year. Laura, your attitude toward change when it comes to uncovering concealed homicides is something I try to emulate. Several times this year I found myself reading your work and nodding along with you, thinking "Yes, Laura!" You are an ideas woman through and through and I am so glad you are pushing this issue forward with me, difficult as it may be sometimes.

Dr. Kelly Palmer's editing and proofreading of chapters also assisted me immeasurably in the final stages of completing this project. I am confident that your feedback has greatly enhanced the style and flair of this, Kelly, and I am so grateful to have had your help. Thank you for restoring my confidence in my writing and for reassuring me that the tone of academic work doesn't always need to be boring. Because of your feedback, I hope I have now officially removed my elbow patches and monocle. I am also grateful for your nonalcoholic wine recommendations. They are all terrible, but they sometimes tricked me into thinking I wasn't so stressed. Thank you.

I must also acknowledge all the police agencies and detectives that I have worked with and hopefully will continue to work with into the future. Detectives and others in the Queensland Police Service (especially the Detective Training Section), South Australian Police, Brevard County Sheriff's Office and Edmonton Police Service have taught me a lot about the issues they face when dealing with possible DA behaviors at death scenes. I am grateful for their openness to share their experience with a researcher. Officers and agencies I have worked with on individual cases or policies have also assisted me with understanding the issues confronting police investigating deaths and I am so appreciative of their willingness to reach out. Symbiotic relationships between police and researchers are absolutely invaluable to this work and benefit many more agencies, detectives and academics beyond us. Thank you and I hope we can continue to collaborate.

Finally, of course, I must acknowledge my colleagues, family and friends. You have all provided such excellent moral support this year, I know that I would not have been able to complete this book without you. Thank you to my colleagues in the School of Justice for being so sure that I would get the ideas on paper in time. I didn't believe you but I was wrong, again. Thank you to my friends for not asking me "how's the book going?" and letting me think about other, happier things every so often. I'm looking at you, Karra – if that is your real name. Rodney, thank you for always making me dinner and listening to my incessant stressing. You poor thing, I cannot imagine what you've been through dealing with me this year. I could promise to relax a bit, but I would be lying, and I think you're stuck with me regardless. Sorry. Team Ferguson, thanks for your unwavering support, as always. I can never repay all the positive energy you've put into every project I undertake, but I will provide one grandchild as a start. After that, no promises.

Note

1 Thanks to a legendary data recovery company, much of the data for this book ended up being saved; however, it took months and I'd frantically rewritten most of it in the meantime.

Abbreviations

CIB	Criminal Investigative Branch
CSS	Crime Scene Staging
DA	Detection Avoidance
DV	Domestic Violence
GO CID	General Office Criminal Investigative Division
IPF	Intimate Partner Femicide
IPH	Intimate Partner Homicide
IPV	Intimate Partner Violence
MDS	Multi-Dimensional Scaling
PCL-R	Psychopathy Checklist Revised
SAA	Smallest Space Analysis

Glossary

Body disposal A type of detection avoidance behavior where offenders leave a victim's body somewhere in order to distance the body from crime scenes, the offender(s) or to conceal it in order to delay its discovery. This may involve luring a live victim to a location or transporting a deceased victim's body to the disposal location

Coercive control In relationships, this is akin to entrapment. A person's strategic course of self-interested behavior intended to reinforce and increase gender-based privilege by dominating their partner's personal life

Complex death investigation A sudden death investigation involving challenges in establishing suspiciousness, manner of death and so on. Results of these investigations may be controversial

Concealed homicide A type of crime scene staging where a homicide is staged to appear as a different manner of death, such as an accident or suicide

Countermeasures A synonym for detection avoidance, behaviors used by offenders to avoid detection or apprehension by police

Crime scene staging A type of detection avoidance, crime scene staging is the deliberate alteration of physical evidence at the location where a crime has actually or allegedly occurred in an effort to simulate events that did not occur. Crime scene staging is intended to mislead authorities or redirect an investigation

CSI Effect The proposition that juries' decisions are being skewed by what they have learned through viewing television shows, such as *CSI – Crime Scene Investigation*, which stylizes forensic procedures

Death investigation A general term used to describe a statutory investigation of a usually sudden, violent or unexpected death, unattended by a physician. The purpose of a death investigation is generally to establish the identity of the decedent, the medical cause of death, the manner of death and whether the death requires criminal investigation. Death investigations are carried out by authorized officials, usually police

Deception A false communication that tends to benefit the communicator

Detection avoidance Behaviors that an offender employs to hide, destroy or manipulate evidence in order to avoid detection or apprehension by police

Equivocal death analysis Determining whether a death was accidental, natural, suicide, homicide or undetermined

Forensic awareness Used as a synonym for detection avoidance, involves an offender changing their modus operandi to prevent evidence being deposited or destroying it after the fact, in an effort to thwart investigative efforts

Goddefroy's method Utilized to determine whether a dead person has been hung up by someone else in the case of an equivocal hanging

Intimate partner femicide Homicides where the victim is a woman and is killed by a current or former intimate partner, including same-sex and extramarital relationships

Intimate partner homicide Homicides where the victim and offender have a current or former intimate relationship, including same-sex and extramarital relationships

Manner of death Established by both medical professionals and death investigators, sometimes independently. Manner of death may be ruled as natural, accidental, suicidal, homicidal or undetermined

Modus operandi Mode of operating, used to describe how offenders perpetrate their crimes

Motivational impairment effect The more motivated a liar is to avoid getting caught, the more likely it is their behavior will give their lies away

Posing Positioning of a homicide victim's body to make the scene appear to be something that it is not, designed to leave the victim in a sexually degrading position

Psychopathy A general term referring to a chronic disorder involving abnormal or violent social behavior. Psychopaths are characterized by persistent antisocial behavior, lack of empathy and remorse, manipulativeness and egotistical traits. Psychopathy is not a psychological diagnosis, but its measurement is commonly used in criminal justice settings

Rational choice theory Attributes criminal behavior to reasoning criminals, who weigh rewards and punishments before choosing between different courses of action

Selective impulsivity Where psychopathic offenders may choose not to inhibit impulsive aggression when the stakes are low; however, where an impulsive response is likely to result in severe consequences, they may make very rapid decisions to resist the aggressive behavior or delay their reaction

Socratic method A method of teaching where the expert gives no new information but asks a sequence of questions, through answering which the pupil discovers the desired knowledge

Solvability factors Those pieces of information discovered within the crime event that assist in catching the perpetrator and closing the case

Staging A short form for crime scene staging

Sudden death investigation A statutory investigation occurring after a death which is unattended by a physician, usually a violent or unexpected death. See death investigation

Suspicious death Not necessarily a criminal death, but a death requiring a thorough investigation of criminality to determine whether a full homicide investigation is required

Verbal staging Where an offender makes self-initiated contact with police to report a homicide victim as a missing person in an effort to avoid investigative scrutiny

1 A continuing history of research into detection avoidance

This chapter begins by introducing detection avoidance (DA) in homicide cases as a behavior seen and discussed throughout history in fictional, criminal justice practitioner-focused and academic literature. Definitions of the key terms are introduced and notable debates in the literature are outlined. Early treatment of the subject of DA and crime scene staging (CSS) by notable historical voices are explored, including recommendations for how to investigate these death scenes properly and thoroughly. Finally, more recent discussions by both practitioner and academic authors are summarized, with specific reference to the scarcity of the literature available on DA in homicide in general. Given the challenges posed with discriminating between offender behaviors when little theoretical work exists, literature on CSS is introduced to fill the gap.

Lying and manipulating evidence has been used by motivated offenders to escape suspicion of criminal behavior for centuries. In William Shakespeare's *The Tragedy of Macbeth* (1892), written in the early 1600s, Macbeth and his wife murder King Duncan, clean their hands and smear his blood on the watchmen to give the illusion that they themselves were not the guilty parties. Shakespeare provides the following description (1892, ACT II, SCENE II):

LADY MACBETH
Go get some water,
And wash this filthy witness from your hand. Why did you bring these daggers from the place? They must lie there: go carry them; and smear The sleepy grooms with blood.
MACBETH
I'll go no more:

I am afraid to think what I have done; Look on't again I dare not.

Along with motivated offenders, investigators responsible for investigating sudden, suspicious or complex deaths have been aware of the potential for countermeasures to be used by offenders for centuries as well. Investigators have tried to combat these offender efforts with various investigative philosophies, forensic techniques, policy, training and the like. The earliest description of the challenge DA behaviors pose in criminal investigations was provided by Dr. Hans Gross (1936). Gross referred to the clues which give away attempts at DA as 'defects'. He writes (p. 433):

> The "defects of the situation" are just those contradictions, those improbabilities, which occur when one desires to represent the situation as something quite different from what it really is, and this with the very best intentions and the purest belief that one has worked with all the forethought, craft and consideration imaginable.

These defects, which have also been called incongruities, inconsistencies, deceits, improbabilities and paradoxes, and how they may be recognized have received little attention in the academic literature. Sudden death investigators, be they a law enforcement officer, a forensic scientist, a pathologist or an accident reconstructionist, have therefore mostly used idiosyncratic methods and gut instincts to identify and explain DA behaviors. This book centers around filling this gap by describing and theorizing, in a scholarly manner, the use of DA by offenders. It examines and critiques how these types of behaviors have been researched, identifies key challenges posed by the use of DA and opportunities to overcome these, as well as examines how training may reduce the impact these offender behaviors have on sudden, suspicious or complex death investigations.

Definitions

DA by offenders has also been referred to as using *countermeasures*, *forensic awareness* behaviors, evidence manipulation, *precautionary acts* and *adaptive behaviors* in the forensic psychology and criminology literature (Neimeyer, Pepper, & Salfati, 2008; Turvey, 2008). Here it will mostly be called DA, but other terms are also used where appropriate. DA behaviors are those which an offender employs to hide, destroy or manipulate evidence in order to avoid detection or apprehension by police (Beauregard & Bouchard, 2010; Beauregard & Martineau, 2012, 2014; Canter, 1989; Davies, 1992; Salfati & Haratsis, 2001).

Forensic psychologists and criminologists have long recognized the use of DA and the challenges they pose to investigations. Referring to these behaviors as *forensic awareness*, the first contemporary treatment of the issue appeared in 1989 when psychologist David Canter discussed the importance of identifying, through crime scene behaviors, whether police had previously questioned offenders. Canter discussed the concept from an investigative psychology standpoint, indicating that those crime scenes evidencing DA are likely to involve experienced offenders, especially in sexual assault cases. Also studying sexual assault, Davies (1992) went on to define forensic awareness as an offender changing their modus operandi to prevent evidence being deposited or destroying it after the fact, in an effort to thwart investigative efforts. Davies (1992) noted that there are several possible expressions of forensic awareness in an offender's modus operandi, including avoiding interruptions, protecting their identity, avoiding reporting and ensuring a safe getaway.

It is not uncommon in many homicide cases for the offender to engage in DA (Turvey, 2008). Turvey terms these behaviors 'precautionary acts' (Turvey, 2008, p. 212) and describes them as "behaviors that offenders commit before, during or after an offense that are consciously intended to confuse, hamper, or defeat investigative or forensic efforts for the purposes of concealing their identity, their connection to the crime, or the crime itself". A few examples include using a mask, clothing or disguise to conceal physical features of the offender; choosing a secluded or less travelled location for the offense; using gloves to prevent the transfer of fingerprints or biological fluids; staging the crime scene; and so on (Turvey, 2008).

CSS is one of many forms of DA offenders may carry out in order to distance themselves from a homicide, and this form of DA has received the most attention in the academic literature. CSS is also not uncommon in death investigations, although perhaps less so than DA more broadly (Geberth, 2006; Hazelwood & Napier, 2004; Schlesinger Gardenier, Jarvis, & Sheehan-Cook, 2012; Turvey, 2008). CSS is defined as the deliberate alteration of physical evidence in an effort to simulate events or offenses that did not occur, for the purpose of misleading authorities. For example, after killing a person an offender may relocate the deceased's body into a car, position it as if the victim was driving and send the car into a body of water to give the impression the victim died in an automobile accident. In such a case, the act of relocating the body, positioning it in the car and driving into the water would be considered acts of CSS, or just *staging*. Homicides involving staging have also been referred to in the literature as *concealed homicides*, where a murder is made to look like a noncriminal death (e.g., a suicide or accident). This terminology is especially popular in the literature on intimate partner homicide (IPH) and intimate partner femicide (IPF); however, the behavior being referred to is better known as CSS in the broader literature on death and homicide investigation.

The easiest way to conceptualize the difference between DA more broadly and CSS is to note that, where DA generally involves taking something away or preventing something from being left at the scene, staging involves an attempt to prevent offender identification by adding something to the scene to give the impression that something else has occurred. Important in both definitions is noting the motivation behind the countermeasures – where they are carried out for the purpose of thwarting investigators or investigations rather than for some other reason.

Early works

Despite DA being somewhat common (Geberth, 1996; Gross, 1936; Hazelwood & Napier, 2004; Turvey, 2000), the forensic criminology, psychology and science communities know very little about it. The following section outlines what has been discovered to date in the study of DA in death investigations.

Dr. Hans Gross, arguably the most influential early scholar in criminal investigation, is one of the few who has confronted the issue of DA and CSS directly. Regardless of his works being nearly a century old, Gross maintains some of the most detailed and relevant discussions of the use of DA by offenders. In his seminal text on criminal investigation, Gross (1936) mostly provides practical advice to investigators responsible for making decisions about possible suspicious deaths. He notes that death investigators need to be constantly aware of the fact that offenders commonly use countermeasures to evade detection, and therefore investigators should examine each case through a lens of relative skepticism. He advises that by doing so, the investigating officer can determine the contradictions, paradoxes and the defects that lead the officer to discover the "grand blunder" which, he explains, "the most experienced and crafty criminal rarely fails to commit" (p. 433). To uncover this, he advises investigators to consider what each circumstance of the case would signify if the crime actually occurred the way it presents as well as what it would signify if the crime were a false report or something else, such as a concealed homicide.

In O'Connell and Soderman's (1936) manual on investigating deaths, there is some reference to what these authors refer to as *simulated* crime scenes in their discussion of distinguishing homicides from suicides. Their simulated scenes are akin to CSS and the discussion of them provides a useful starting point for thinking about this type of DA in particular. O'Connell and Soderman's (1936) work stresses the need to identify inconsistencies in injuries and wound patterns to the victim, which do not correspond with the alleged narrative or facts of the case. Similar to other books on the issue from around this time, O'Connell and Soderman (1936) do not provide reference to any scholarly research, and practical recommendations for how to do death investigations dominate. These authors offer detailed and specific procedures for investigating scenes of fatal shootings, hangings, strangulations, slit or stab wounds, chop wounds, traffic accidents, falls, drownings and poisoning. The specific recommendations given for examining each of these types of deaths need not be summarized in this introduction (see Ferguson, 2011, for a more detailed summary). However, their discussion of *Goddefroy's method* warrants noting as it is one of the only specific techniques ever proposed which may address whether evidence has been staged based on fixed indicators. O'Connell and Soderman (1936) propose that *Goddefroy's method* can be utilized to determine whether a dead person has been hung up by someone else in the case of an equivocal hanging (e.g., one where it is difficult to determine between homicide, suicide and accident). O'Connell and Soderman (1936) also note the challenge posed by injuries of this type when attempting to determine manner of death (i.e., determine whether the death was a result of natural, accidental, suicidal, homicidal or undetermined causes). They state (1936, p. 264):

> By hanging a murdered person practically the same marks as those caused by strangulation may be produced. There is no sure way, either by autopsy or by microscopic examination of the marks, of determining whether a person was hanged after death or not...In most cases strangulation will be used to simulate suicide, although poisoning and especially choking may have caused death...The examination of the rope may reveal most important information. This question has been studied by the Belgian detective, E. Goddefroy, and such examinations have led, in the last few years, to the solution of quite a few crimes on the Continent.

Although treated much more briefly, the work of O'Hara and Osterburg (1972, reprinted from 1949) is also historically noteworthy to a discussion of DA and CSS. These authors state that miscarriages of justice can occur when an offender seeks to frame someone else and manipulates evidence at a homicide scene to indicate that person as the offender. Being a text on criminalistics, this work describes how manipulated evidence can be detected using technologies available in the forensic sciences in the middle of the 20th century. The authors also highlight themes related to power of the situation, the cognitive load weighing on offenders using DA and DA as a type of deception – all three of which will be addressed in subsequent chapters throughout this book. O'Hara and Osterburg state (1972, p. 683):

> The laboratory in the majority of these cases will be able to detect the simulated evidence. The reasons for this are simple. The criminal is frequently suffering an emotional disturbance when committing the crime and while substituting the fraudulent clue materials. This in addition to the fact that he usually has little, if any, experience in the appearance or requisites of physical evidence, enables the deception to be uncovered.

In their book on the various methods of crime scene examination, Svensson and Wendel (1974) stress the importance of systematic analyses and proper comparisons of physical evidence in order to recognize and identify DA. In a passage echoing O'Hara and Osterburg (1972) and Gross (1936), they note that the frailties of any perpetrator of homicide can be used to the advantage of the investigation (p. 292):

> Even when the murderer has carefully planned the crime and taken all imaginable precautions to avoid leaving traces, they are still found. As

> a rule, the murderer comes to a sudden realization of the terrible results of his deed after the killing. He may then lose his head completely and try to obliterate the evidence of his act, but in his confused state of mind only works against himself by leaving new clues.

In terms of resolving equivocal deaths, Svensson and Wendel (1974) recommend that investigators examining these scenes must always err on the side of caution and suspect the worst – that is, if there is any confusion, it is less harmful to rule a suicide as a homicide than vice versa. In terms of how to actually go about determining manner of death, they stress the importance of a thorough and detailed investigation, noting the possibility of CSS as a specific form of DA (p. 293):

> A clever murderer may very well arrange an accident, or make the death appear to be due to suicide. Such a murderer has every opportunity of arranging matters to deceive those who treat their task of investigating the circumstances too lightly. But a systematic and accurate investigation will reveal the homicidal intent.

Although not cited anywhere, Svensson and Wendel's (1974) advice is reminiscent of Gross's (1936) discussion of the defects of the situation. Svensson and Wendel (1974) also provide a list of inquiries that they recommend the investigator make early on in the investigation in order to facilitate the accurate determination of the manner of death. They advise that everything in the scene be documented, especially the position of any clothing, its folds, twists, creases, tears, buttonholes, fasteners, stains, size and so on. Bloodstains, smears, spatters, froth and droplets on the body or clothing must also be examined and photographed. The absence of blood should also be documented as an offender may have cleaned a victim after death. Interestingly, despite being given nearly 50 years ago, much of this advice is similar to that provided in contemporary policy reform recommendations for death investigators today, as discussed in Chapter 7, suggesting, perhaps, the message still has yet to be received. Svensson and Wendel (1974) additionally mention the importance of utilizing a qualified forensic pathologist to determine the cause and manner of death and warn against equating experience with expertise. This advice is also reiterated in the last chapter of this book.

Contemporary works

Along with sage advice provided by some of the fathers of modern criminal investigations, there are several contemporary authors who have made noteworthy contributions to understanding the use of DA in death investigation as well. These works can be broken into those addressing DA more generally and those discussing how to investigate deaths involving possible

CSS. The small literature on DA generally is comprised of empirical studies in the form of academic journal articles. These studies have been generally descriptive, and their specific findings will be presented in more detail in Chapter 2. The literature on CSS is most often found in criminal investigation manuals, with a small section or chapter devoted to manipulated evidence and staging. Despite treatment of the issue being practitioner-focused and not necessarily evidence-based, these authors provide a useful starting point for theorizing the challenges and impacts of offenders' use of DA.

DA literature

After Canter (1989) and Davies (1992) described adaptive behaviors and what they mean to profiling offenders, discussion on the use of DA by homicide offenders was scant until about 2005. At this point, discussions of offender countermeasures were reinvigorated when they were couched within broader concerns regarding the *CSI Effect*. One type of CSI Effect is what Cole and Diosa-Villa (2007) have termed the "police chief's version" of the effect – theorizing that if jurors are learning about forensic techniques through forensic science media, then so too might offenders. The evidence for this type of CSI Effect is mixed and will be discussed in more detail in Chapter 5.

For now it is important to note that controversy surrounding the impact of CSI-type media on offending led to several authors reinventing the concept of DA and measuring how often offenders attempt to thwart investigative efforts, how successful these efforts are and why (Beauregard & Bouchard, 2010; Beauregard & Martineau, 2014; Brown & Keppel, 2012; Ferguson & McKinley, in press; Neimeyer et al., 2008; Salfati & Haratsis, 2001). As mentioned, the specific results of these empirical studies are discussed in the next chapter and elsewhere in this book. Here it is worthwhile observing that despite the discussion being very practice-focused historically, the few discussions of DA available from the last 10–15 years are more often authored by academic researchers than practitioners. This is an interesting gap in the practitioner-focused literature and demonstrates an important shift in the knowledge base surrounding DA. Where previously DA was described and discussed almost exclusively by investigators and forensic scientists based on their experiences, less has been explicitly said by this group in recent years. Today, discussions of DA in homicides are more so based on empirical research carried out by academics. The exception to this surrounds the literature on CSS, which, at least for homicide cases, enjoyed some discussion by practitioners around the turn of the 21st century as well as more recent study by academics. While these discussions are of CSS overtly, similar to the historical literature, many of the findings and recommendations described are relevant to DA more broadly as well.

CSS literature

Much of the literature specific to CSS surrounds how homicides potentially involving CSS should be investigated, the most common forms of CSS utilized by offenders and less often, the types of homicides in which staging is commonly found. Since there are few of these discussions, each can be briefly described with reference to the key themes reported by each set of authors. Specific empirical findings, including rates of CSS and common behaviors employed by offenders, are covered in Chapter 2.

The FBI's Crime Classification Manual (1992, 2006) was the first investigative handbook to discuss the use of DA by offenders contemporarily. In this manual, Douglas and Munn (1992) and Douglas and Douglas (2006) offer a list of questions for investigators to ask and things they should be cognizant of in determining when evidence at a death scene has been manipulated, including red flags both at the scene and in the laboratory. They first consider though that often the inconsistencies which are noticed by investigators are due to the fact that the offender stages evidence at the crime to appear as he/she *thinks* it should appear, not as it necessarily would if the scenario was legitimate. For instance, if concealing an IPH as a suicide, the offender may have no insight into how a suicide usually presents, having never seen one previously. The offender will be forced to stage the scene to resemble how they think a real suicide would look, all while under the stress of having committed or being about to commit a homicide. Because of this stress and the associated cognitive load, the pieces may not fit together in a logical way, evidencing Gross' (1936) defects.

Hazelwood and Napier (2004) studied CSS by canvassing 20 consultants who have testified as experts or worked cases involving staged evidence. The rationale behind this study is consistent with other authors (e.g., Geberth, 1996, discussed below), who opine that the frequency of staging behaviors is on the rise due to the effect of mass media and the resulting CSI Effect. Hazelwood and Napier (2004) found that investigators most commonly saw CSS in nonfatal sexual assault cases (e.g., false reports), followed by staging homicides as burglary-related or robbery-related crimes, staging the manner of death (concealed homicides) and staging homicides as sexually related crimes.

FBI agents Hazelwood and Napier (2004, p. 751) state that staging can be done in order to mislead the investigator as to "(a) the manner of death (i.e., homicide, suicide, accident, natural or other), (b) the cause of death (i.e., the medical reason for the death) or (c) the motive for the original act (i.e., greed, anger-revenge, attention, game playing or other)", and that the motivation behind these goals is either self-preservation or embarrassment-shame. The first motivation (self-preservation) is that which is typically endorsed in the other CSS literature, applying to the perpetrator who wishes to manipulate evidence to avoid detection. The embarrassment-shame motivation is where the offender "is attempting to provide the victim with a degree of dignity or to allow the family to remember the victim in a more generous sense than the original scene would have allowed" (p. 751). This embarrassment-shame motivation is typically not recognized by other scholars and is heavily criticized by Geberth (1996), Turvey (2008) and others. Hazelwood and Napier defend this part of their definition, saying that "when the location has been intentionally rearranged to mislead the investigation as to the means or manner or death, it has been staged, and the classification is certainly applicable" (p. 753). However, most others argue that an act intended, by definition, to avoid embarrassment for the victim or the family is quite a different entity to the criminal behavior of an offender motivated by a desire to avoid detection. Hazelwood and Napier (2004) further note that "sparing the relatives embarrassment or shame should not enter into the decision on whether to categorize or investigate a scene as staged" (p. 753). Though this statement is probably agreeable, the distinction between these two different types of behaviors is paramount, especially considering that sparing shame and embarrassment is not a form of DA. Definitional issues such as this exemplify a key debate in the discussion of DA and CSS. The debate reappears in some of the other works on DA and CSS as well, and its implications are unpacked in Chapter 3.

In the same study, Hazelwood and Napier (2004) provide general commentary for investigators which is similar to that of Douglas and Munn (1992) and Douglas and Douglas (2006). They note that an investigator has two main sources of information on CSS for any given crime, those being the scene and the victim. The same could be said of DA more broadly. In order to determine whether and what inconsistencies are present which may indicate that DA/CSS has been used, they recommend a careful victimology be undertaken. They also propose that there are three areas where contradictions may be discovered: victim-centered, immediate location and distant locations. Hazelwood and Napier (2004) recommend taking a narrative view of the investigation, where observations are compared against the investigators' theories (p. 757):

> All behaviors and other significant facts about the crime are placed in one of these three categories. The investigator then compares what he observes in and across each category with what he would expect to observe in similar situations, basing those expectations on his education, training and experience. In other words, does what he observes make sense? If the investigator observes inconsistencies, they must be explained.

In his book *Practical Homicide Investigation*, Geberth (1996, 2006) examines CSS in the context of equivocal death analyses – those where it is unclear whether a death was a result of accidental, natural, suicidal, homicidal or undetermined causes. He discusses DA in terms of how an investigation should proceed at a death scene of unknown origin. In defining CSS, he notes that it is a "conscious criminal action on the part of an offender to thwart an investigation" (p. 22). He also makes note of the fact that previous authors (e.g., Chancellor & Graham, 2014; Douglas & Douglas, 2006; Douglas & Munn, 1992; Hazelwood & Napier, 2004; Meloy, 2002) have referred to the actions of an embarrassed family member as an effort to stage the scene. Geberth disagrees with this inclusion in the definition and explains that these actions are understandable in the bereaved. However, he maintains that embarrassment-shame-motivated evidence manipulation has a completely different intent, and therefore should be considered a separate behavior.

Without citing any empirical evidence-base for identifying DA, Geberth (1996, p. 23) recommends investigators remember "things are not always what they appear to be" and listen to gut feelings. He notes that in his experience, homicides involving DA are increasing due to the public having better knowledge of death investigations through the media, television, movies and books. In terms of strategies for investigating manipulated death scenes, Geberth (1996, p. 29) provides a checklist to assist detectives. This checklist has been heavily criticized elsewhere for being vague, repetitive and out of order, and therefore it does not need to be reproduced here; however, more will be said of the advantages of using evidence-based checklists as an investigative aid in Chapter 7.

Citing Geberth (1996), Keppel and Weis (2004) discuss the rarity of staging as well as posing of bodies at complex death scenes. These authors first differentiate between staging and posing behaviors, and then give case examples and common characteristics of each. They note (p. 1310) that "posing is not to be confused with staging, because staging refers to manipulation of the scene around the body as well as positioning of the body to make the scene appear to be something that it is not", whereas posing is designed to leave the victim in a position which would be considered sexually degrading. This could be done, according to Keppel and Weis (2004, p. 1310), for one of two reasons: "(1) to shock the finder of the body or police investigators, and (2) for the killer's own pleasure". However, posing a body in a sexually degrading position may also be used as a way of staging the scene. Failure to recognize this fact is problematic as it may lead to exactly what Keppel and Weis warn against – confusing staging for posing.

Despite the narrow scope of the sampling procedure used in Keppel and Weis's (2004) study, the authors conclude "posing a victim's body or staging a murder scene occurs so infrequently that it is unlikely that most violent crime investigators will ever investigate a murder that has been staged or posed". This is contradictory to what others have proposed pertaining to the commonality of these scenes (Geberth, 1996; Gross, 1936; Schlesinger et al., 2012; Turvey, 2000). Keppel and Weis (2004) also note that (p. 1308) "staging a murder scene requires the killer to spend time before the murder, planning its execution". This is again reiterated at the end of the paper (p. 1311): "[placing bodies in unusual positions] requires that the offender spend time planning the events leading up to murder and rearranging the body and crime scene after the victim's death". These statements are not referenced to any previous work or the findings in their study, and given the findings of other works described elsewhere in this book, the necessity for planning of CSS remains controversial.

Upon identifying the lack of systematic research on CSS, Turvey (2000) conducted a basic descriptive study to identify common characteristics associated with staged crime scenes. Despite offering the first empirical study of CSS, Turvey's work was atheoretical, offering little in the way of explanation for these behaviors. The research examined 25 homicide cases in the USA, and because of the link between staged crime scenes and IPH, compared its findings to those found in similar studies of IPH in the USA (Bureau of Justice Statistics, 1998; Mukherjee, Van Winkle, & Zimring, 1983). Turvey's (2000) study found that all offenders had a current or prior family or intimate relationship with their victim, supporting Geberth's (1996) hypothesis that CSS is most commonly used to conceal an offender's close relationship with the victim (Turvey, 2000).

Since Turvey (2000) highlighted the need for a detailed reconstruction to be undertaken in those scenes with possible DA or CSS, Chisum and Turvey (2007) went on to discuss the importance of keeping the science, and forensic science in the efforts of those analyzing and reconstructing complex death scenes. Chisum and Turvey (2007) offer advice to practitioners which is similar in its sentiment to that of the earliest works relating to CSS, especially those of Gross (1936). They propose an investigative philosophy, including using the scientific method, possessing a skeptical mindset and keeping the possibility of evidence manipulation in mind. Interestingly, Chisum and Turvey also note that there are undoubtedly cases where DA or CSS has not been discovered, leading to homicides being misclassified and permanently concealed.

Aside from this mantra of skepticism, Chisum and Turvey (2007) also suggest several queries that the reconstructionist should address within various elements of the scene in order to determine if any evidence has been manipulated. This work was cited in the National Academy of Science's publication entitled *Strengthening Forensic Science in the United States: A Path Forward* (2009), a major credit to its quality and usefulness.

Other than appearing in investigative manuals, research and discussions of DA in the form of CSS have also been the focus of a handful of PhD dissertations. Although the results remain unpublished, in 2007 Eke studied CSS in 48 homicides, finding that intimate partners most commonly stage death scenes, followed by family members and acquaintances (Eke, 2007). This research also discovered that scenes in Canada were most commonly staged to appear as break and enters, accidents or missing people. Eke's (2007) PhD research then compared staged with non-staged IPH cases. Using a psychological perspective, Psychopathy Check-List Revised (PCL-R) scores of offenders were compared, with findings revealing that stagers typically scored higher on this measure than non-stagers. Explanations from the psychopathy literature are discussed and will be examined in detail in Chapters 5 and 6. Eke (2007) found that intimate partner offenders most commonly stage deaths as missing persons and attempt to permanently dispose of the victim's body so that it will not be discovered. This behavior has been referred to as *verbal staging* elsewhere in the literature (Schlesinger et al., 2012), where offenders actively make contact with police in order to appear as a concerned loved one making a missing person's report. The staging is in cleaning up or destroying evidence of the homicide as well as potentially making it appear that a victim has disappeared of their own volition or for some other reason unrelated to the true events.

Pettler's (2011) PhD is discussed in detail in Chapter 3. Pettler (2011) assessed 18 cases of CSS in homicides in North Carolina and published her results in the first book on CSS in 2016. This project was aimed at developing a model of crime scene stagers' behaviors and a methodology for early detection of staging. Pettler's (2011) qualitative thesis sought to establish whether there was a common set of behaviors amongst offenders staging homicides. She found a much lower proportion of victims and offenders who were known to each other or intimate partners in comparison to that found in other works (Ferguson, 2015; Schlesinger et al., 2012). This finding is best explained by the broad definition of CSS employed by Pettler (2011), where behaviors that have elsewhere been defined as DA rather than CSS were included. For example, covering a body to stop it being discovered would generally be considered DA rather than CSS in most other works; however, doing so was defined as a staging behavior in Pettler's (2011) thesis. More will be said of the impact of this definition on categorizing and studying DA behaviors in Chapter 3.

Ferguson's (2011) doctoral research studied 141 homicide cases involving CSS. This project examined the state of the field in detail to explain differences in CSS perpetrated across different staging types. Common elements of the crimes, victim and perpetrator characteristics and specific features were assessed. More will be said of the specifics of this analysis in Chapters 2 and 3. Basic findings of this project, published in part in 2015, included the presence of multiple victims and offenders; a previous relationship between parties involved; and victims discovered in their own home, often by the offender (Ferguson, 2015). Ferguson (2011) was determined that different type of staged scenes – staged burglaries, suicides, accidents and car accidents – display differently with separate indicators and common features, at least at a descriptive level. Ferguson's (2011) results suggest offenders use few behaviors to show the false narrative, despite the credibility additional behaviors may have offered their façade. While this research was largely descriptive, its publication in 2015 was the first peer-reviewed, published study to examine the specific features of staged crime scenes and provided the largest sample studied to date. This study highlighted the necessity to explain why only some cases involve DA and CSS, given the likelihood that most offenders would ultimately prefer not to be discovered by police and held accountable. Why do some choose to manipulate the evidence and redirect the investigation while others do not? This question will provide a recurring theme in the coming chapters and will be discussed in detail in Chapters 5 and 6.

Finally, in one of the only empirical studies of DA involving collaboration between academic and practitioner-focused researchers, Schlesinger and colleagues (2012) studied CSS in a sample of 79 staged homicide crime scenes in the USA to determine how often these types of behaviors were perpetrated, the types of homicides involved, levels of effort expended by the offender(s) and the related motivations (Schlesinger et al., 2012).

Schlesinger et al.'s (2012) major findings included the prevalence of multiple victims and the rudimentary nature of the staging efforts. Types of homicides (domestic, non-serial sexual, serial sexual and general felony) were separated, and CSS within each type was examined. It was determined that domestic homicides often involve verbal staging whereas non-domestic homicides more often involve arson. Relationship patterns between victims and offenders were discussed and it was found that there is often an intimate or familial relationship involved, as was indicated by the higher level of staging in domestic cases. Although limited by sampling perhaps the most complex death scenes, those held by the FBI's behavioral analysis unit, Schlesinger et al.'s work provides the first robust indication of the prevalence of staging in homicides, occurring in 8% of cases sampled. Given the conservation definition of CSS used, the prevalence of DA more broadly would expectedly be much higher. More importantly though, the combined academic rigor and real-world usefulness of this study exemplify the contributions that can be made to understanding DA when research collaborations between police and academic partners are successful. This, too, will be a reoccurring issue discussed in the coming chapters of this book.

Conclusion

The use of DA by homicide offenders has been talked about for centuries. Forensic psychologists, criminologists, police and medical professionals have written about how offenders may attempt to avoid detection and how these efforts can be uncovered by police. Despite these discussions, little empirical work is available which theorizes the use of DA and explains why it is used by some offenders and not others, or indeed in some offenses but not others committed by the same person. This chapter has introduced some of the key themes which will thread through this book, including the problems with defining and discriminating between DA and CSS, the apparent lack of communication and collaboration between practitioners and researchers, the role of intimate partner violence, the offender's cognitive load and mental health and the use of DA as a form of deception. All of these issues will be addressed in detail in the coming chapters. Particular reference will be paid to explaining how, when and why DA behaviors are used by offenders, their impact and opportunities for overcoming the challenges they pose in sudden, suspicious and/or complex death investigations.

References

Beauregard, E., & Bouchard, M. (2010). Cleaning up your act: Forensic awareness as a detection avoidance strategy. *Journal of Criminal Justice, 38*, 1160–1166. doi: 10.1016/j.jcrimjus.2010.09.004

Beauregard, E., & Martineau, M. (2012). A descriptive study of sexual homicide in Canada: Implications for police investigation. *International Journal of Offender Therapy and Comparative Criminology, 57*(12), 1454–1476. doi: 10.1177/0306624X12456682

Beauregard, E., & Martineau, M. (2014). No body, no crime? The role of forensic awareness in avoiding police detection in cases of sexual homicide. *Journal of Criminal Justice, 42*, 213–220. doi: 10.1016/j.jcrimjus.2013.06.007

Brown, K., & Keppel, R. (2012). Child abduction murder: The impact of forensic evidence on solvability. *Journal of Forensic Sciences, 57*(2), 353–353. doi:10.1111/j.1556-4029.2011.01970.x

Bureau of Justice Statistics (BJS). (1998). Violence by intimates: Analysis of data on crimes by current or former spouses, boyfriends, and girlfriends In B. Turvey (Ed.), *Criminal profiling: An introduction to behavioral evidence analysis* (2nd ed.). London: Academic Press (2002).

Canter, D. (1989). Offender profiling. *The Psychologist, 2*(1), 12–16.

Chancellor, A., & Graham, G. (2014). Staged crime scenes: Crime scene clues to suspect misdirection of the investigation. *Investigative Sciences Journal, 6*(1), 19–35.

Chisum, W. J., & Turvey, B. E. (2007). A history of crime reconstruction. In W. J. Chisum & B. E. Turvey (Eds.), *Crime reconstruction* (pp. 1–35). London, UK: Academic Press.

Cole, S., & Diosa-Villa, R. (2007). *CSI* and its effects: Media, juries and the burden of proof. *New England Law Review, 41*, 435–469. Accessed October 31, 2016 from: http://ssrn.com/abstract=1023258

Davies, A. (1992). Rapists' behavior: A three aspect model as a basis for analysis and the identification of serial crime. *Forensic Science International, 55*, 173–194.

Douglas, J., & Douglas, L. (2006). The detection of staging, undoing and personation at the crime scene. In J. Douglas, A. W. Burgess, A. G. Burgess, & R. K. Ressler (Eds.), *Crime classification manual* (2nd ed., pp. 31–44). San Francisco, CA: Jossey-Bass.

Douglas, J., & Munn, C. (1992). The detection of staging and personation at the crime scene. In J. Douglas, A. W. Burgess, A. G. Burgess, & R. K. Ressler (Eds.), *Crime classification manual* (pp. 249–258). San Francisco, CA: Jossey-Bass.

Eke, A. (2001). *Staging in cases of homicide: Offender, victim and offence characteristics* (Unpublished doctoral dissertation). University of Toronto, Toronto, Canada.

Ferguson, C. (2011). *The defects of the situation: An examination of staged crime scenes* (Unpublished doctoral dissertation). Bond University, Gold Coast Australia.

Ferguson, C. (2015). Staged homicides: An examination of common features of faked burglaries, suicides, accidents and car accidents. *Journal of Police and Criminal Psychology, 30*(3), 139–157. doi: 10.1007/s11896-014-9154-1

Ferguson, C., & McKinley, A. (in press). The role of detection avoidance behaviour in solving Australian homicides: A proposed framework. *Salus Journal.*

Geberth, V. J. (1996). The Staged Crime Scene. *Law and Order Magazine, February,* 89–92.

Geberth, V. J. (2006). *Practical homicide investigation: Tactics, procedures and forensic techniques* (4th ed.). Boca Raton, FL: CRC Press.

Gross, H. (1936). *Criminal investigation.* London, UK: Sweet & Maxwell.

Hazelwood, R., & Napier, M. (2004). Crime scene staging and its detection. *International Journal of Offender Therapy and Comparative Criminology, 48,* 744–759.

Keppel, R., & Weis, J. (2004). The rarity of "unusual" dispositions of victim bodies: Staging and posing. *Journal of Forensic Science, 49,* 1308–1312.

Meloy, J. (2002). Spousal homicide and the subsequent staging of a sexual homicide at a distant location. *Journal of Forensic Science, 47,* 395–398.

Mukherjee, S., VanWinkle, B., & Zimring, F. (1983). Intimate violence: A study of intersexual homicide in Chicago. In Turvey, B. (Ed.), *Criminal profiling: An introduction to behavioral evidence analysis* (2nd ed.). London: Academic Press (2002).

National Academy of Science. (2009). *Strengthening forensic science in the United States: A path forward.* National Research Council. https://www.ncjrs.gov/pdffiles1/nij/grants/228091.pdf

Neimeyer, E., Pepper, K., & Salfati, G. (2008). *Avoiding detection: An examination of adaptive and maladaptive behaviors in serial homicide.* Paper presented at the American Society of Criminology Annual Meeting, St. Louis, MO.

O'Connell, J., & Soderman, H. (1936). *Modern criminal investigation.* New York: Funk & Wagnalls.

O'Hara, C., & Osterburg, J. (1972). *An introduction to criminalistics.* Bloomington: Indiana University Press.

Pettler, L. (2011). *Crime scene behaviors of crime scene stagers* (Unpublished doctoral thesis). Capella University, Minneapolis, MN.

Salfati, G., & Haratsis, E. (2001). Greek homicide: A behavioral examination of offender crime scene actions. *Homicide Studies, 5*(4), 355–362. doi: 10.1177/1088767901005004006

Schlesinger, L., Gardenier, A., Jarvis, J., & Sheehan-Cook, J. (2012). Crime scene staging in homicide. *Journal of Police and Criminal Psychology.* doi: 10.1007/s11896-012-9114-6

Shakespeare, W. (1892). *The Tragedy of Macbeth.* London: Harper. Retrieved 5 May, 2010 from http:// extra.shu.ac.uk/emls/iemls/resour/mirrors/rbear/shake/macbeth.html

Svensson, A., & Wendel, O. (1974). *Techniques of crime scene investigation* (2nd ed.). New York: American Elsevier.

Turvey, B. (2000). Staged crime scenes: A preliminary study of 25 cases. *Journal of Behavioral Profiling, 1*(3), 1–15.

Turvey, B. (2008). *Criminal profiling: An introduction to behavioral evidence analysis* (3rd ed.). London: Academic Press.

2 The basics of detection avoidance in homicide

Whether, when and which DA behaviors a homicide offender uses runs the gamut depending on the victim and offender relationship and the offender's experience. This chapter outlines the rates of DA in homicide cases, common behaviors employed by offenders and crime types where they are typically seen. Particular types of DA are specifically focused on CSS and body disposal. The importance of examining victim and offender relationships in both the investigation and research of these types of DA are discussed, indicating that rates, relationships and impacts may vary across relationship types. Intimate partner homicides, serial sexual homicides and criminal enterprise homicides involving body disposal are each compared to examine the different constellations of DA behaviors involved in each of these case types. Finally, the impact of DA on homicide investigations is discussed and a specific framework for how these behaviors impact on homicide solvability is proposed. Broad effects include an increase in police resources required to investigate and resolve these deaths; negative implications for family members and detectives involved in these cases; and challenges to whether deaths involving DA are correctly recognized as suspicious, and how quickly. However, the use of DA also provides opportunities to investigators, which are similarly discussed.

Studying DA in homicide cases is of interest to criminologists, forensic scientists, coroners, police and psychologists for a number of reasons. This is because, although previous research has indicated that only a minority of offenders utilize DA behaviors to evade detection by police, there are numerous case examples and research findings suggesting DA can make suspicious death investigations significantly more difficult and resource intensive to investigate and resolve (Beauregard & Bouchard, 2010; Beauregard & Martineau, 2014; Brown & Keppel, 2008; Salfati & Haratsis, 2001). Recent studies show that use of DA by offenders hinders investigations by adding layers of complexity (e.g., multiple crime scenes), if not preventing the crime being solved (Beauregard & Martineau, 2014; Ferguson & McKinley, in press). The CSS literature adds that when looking at cases individually, any one forensically aware and criminally sophisticated offender can create major difficulties for investigators (Geberth, 2015). This impacts on whether suspicious deaths are recognized as such, and how quickly; whether families feel satisfied with how police and courts handled the death of their loved one; the amount of public resources spent on discovering and stopping offenders; and the morale of police investigators.

Before discussing how and why some offenders choose to use DA behaviors during commission of the homicide, the rates of DA, common behaviors employed and crime types where it is typically seen are introduced.

Rates of DA

Research literature examining DA in general is scarce, and only a handful of studies focus on DA in homicide specifically. Most instead focus on nonfatal sexual assault. The homicide research in existence draws important findings on the impact of DA on homicide investigations in those cases where it occurs. For example, in 2001, Salfati and Haratsis examined 210 solved and unsolved single offender, single victim homicides in Greece. They measured two forms of DA: whether forensic evidence was left at the crime scene and whether arson was used to destroy evidence. Evidence was left and discovered at the scene in 78% of solved cases and 32% of unsolved cases, indicating that the remaining 22% and 68%, respectively, may have involved DA. There was a statistically significant difference between solved and unsolved cases in terms of whether DA was utilized by offenders, indicating the potential value of using DA from a perpetrator's perspective. On average, Salfati and Haratsis's (2001) study shows that nearly half of all cases studied involved DA of some sort, or 45% of homicides studied.

Focusing on more experienced homicide offenders, in 2008 Neimeyer, Pepper and Salfati examined 85 serial homicide cases involving 17 offenders. In this sample of murderers, less than 20% used what the authors refer to as *adaptive behaviors* to avoid detection. To unpack the DA behaviors used by offenders, a number of discrete DA behaviors were measured. These included preparing in advance, hiding, covering and cleaning the body, arson, abducting victims in darkness and CSS. Differences in rates observed between this study and Salfati and Haratsis' (2001) examination of Greek homicides may be a product of relationships between serial offenders and victims (more often strangers). Alternatively, the difference may have to do with the absence of evidence in the Greek sample being chocked up to DA by the offender rather than situational or investigative factors (e.g., how thorough searches for evidence might have been).

Highlighting the importance of accounting for homicide type in studying rates of DA, Brown and Keppel studied 347 child murders from the USA in 2012 and found higher rates of DA than both Salfati and Haratsis (2001) and Neimeyer, Pepper and Salfati (2008). In this sample, more than half of the offenders (53%) destroyed evidence, meaning the majority of offenders used some type of DA. This may be due to more offenders being known to victims in child murders, and thus more offenders being motivated to employ countermeasures. In this sample, particular DA behaviors were broken down and rates reported separately. Results showed that the offenders sampled most commonly destroyed evidence by cleaning (7.8%), hiding or burying (3.8%), burning (3.4%), throwing away (2.7%), removing from the scene (2.5%), other (2.1%) and cutting up (0.9%).

So far, rates of DA involving offenders with various relationships to victims suggest around half of homicide offenders attempt to thwart investigative efforts in some fashion.

Following on from these studies, Beauregard and Martineau (2014) studied 350 Canadian homicides, measuring 16 different aspects of DA, which they referred to as *forensic awareness* (see Chapter 1 for a discussion of this term). It should be noted that while this is the most comprehensive study of DA in homicide cases to date, unlike some of the previous authors described, Beauregard and Martineau focused on one homicide type, sexual homicides, regardless of an offender's experience or the number of victims involved in each incident. They determined that 45.7% ($n = 160$) of offenders sampled carried out at least one countermeasure, either before or after the homicide. Beauregard and Martineau (2014) also reported on rates of particular DA behaviors evidenced in their sample. The found that, of the total offenders, 30.6% destroyed evidence, 11.1% disposed of the victim's body, 4.3% protected their identity, 11.4% acted on the victim or environment (e.g., by locking them in or tying them up), 0.9% staged the crime scene and 12% used *other* behaviors, such as securing an alibi, using a lookout and so on. When DA was used by offenders in the sexual homicide cases sampled, the majority of offenders (24.9% of total) used only one behavior to avoid detection – such as destroying evidence, but not also disposing of the body or anything else. Such a finding suggests that, at least in sexual homicides, while nearly half of offenders use some form of DA, the behaviors employed are few, and therefore offender efforts are likely to be relatively unsophisticated in most cases. Reasons for the lack of more DA behaviors being used despite their potential benefit to offenders will be explored briefly below, and in more detail in Chapter 6 on explaining DA.

DA strategies commonly employed

Recall from Chapter 1, in the early conceptualizations of DA, Davies (1992) noted that there are several types of DA possible in an offender's MO, including avoiding interruptions, protecting their identity, avoiding reporting and ensuring a safe getaway. Two decades later, Beauregard and Martineau (2014) built upon this work, similarly discussing several ways that DA could manifest before, after or during a homicide. They noted that offenders may be better able to carry out DA behaviors prior to the homicide as opposed to following it, especially when destroying evidence or cleaning up delays the offender's departure from the crime scene (Beauregard & Martineau, 2014). Beauregard and Bouchard (2010) studied DA in sexual assault cases where the victim survived. In support of pre-offense DA being easier than post-offense, they found that few sexual assault offenders who showed pre-offense DA also evidenced post-offense DA. However, Beauregard and Bouchard's (2010) study examined only those cases involving sexual violence which resulted in the criminal conviction of an offender. In these types of cases, it is more likely that victims and offenders are strangers or acquaintances rather than involved in an intimate or personal relationship.[1] This being so, in cases involving a conviction, offenders may have unprotected or limited access to the crime scene (such as the victim's home). In such a situation, remaining at a victim's home or a public location with the victim to destroy evidence could be considered risky by offenders, as they may be caught or witnessed. Instead, offenders may choose to prepare in advance to avoid detection, so that DA behaviors can be explained as innocent if they are witnessed before the crime, or the offense can be aborted or postponed. Post-offense DA may be less attractive or unnecessary for these sexual offenders. A similar reduction of post-offense DA behaviors may not be borne out in other homicide (or crime) types where offenders have a greater ability to move in and out of crime scenes with fewer associated high risks. A useful example is in intimate partner homicides where the victim and offender share (or shared) the same residence. In these cases, offenders are more likely to have unlimited and legitimate access to the crime scene; they may also know how and when a scene is monitored by guardians and when it is not. This access and intimate knowledge thus decreases the risk of offenders being witnessed by others carrying out DA behaviors, and therefore could increase the attractiveness of post-offense DA. Evidently, acknowledging victim and offender relationships is pertinent to explaining and predicting the types of DA behaviors used by offenders as well as when they are employed relative to the homicide.

Unfortunately, though, other than these limited discussions of types of behaviors engaged in mostly sexual homicides, very few researchers have examined in detail what type of DA behaviors are commonly employed by offenders and under what circumstances they are likely to occur. This is a notable gap in the literature, especially considering the argument that these types of behaviors can be a hindrance to successful criminal investigations (Beauregard & Bouchard, 2010; Durnal, 2010; Salfati & Haratsis, 2001; Stevens, 2008). The exception to this lack of attention in the literature surrounds CSS, which, at least for homicide cases, has been researched in greater detail than any other DA behavior.

Crime scene staging as DA

As described in Chapter 1, CSS is a type of DA (Beauregard & Martineau, 2014; Davies, 1992; Neimeyer, Pepper, & Salfati, 2008). It refers to the deliberate alteration of physical evidence at the location where a crime has actually or allegedly occurred in an effort to simulate events that did not occur. This is intended to mislead authorities or redirect an investigation (Chisum & Turvey, 2007; Ferguson, 2015; Geberth, 2015). Hazelwood and Napier (2004) add there is also verbal staging, where an offender makes self-initiated contact with police to report a homicide victim as a missing person in an effort to avoid investigative scrutiny. Cases of verbal staging may also involve manipulation of the physical evidence; however, intent to redirect an investigation must be present. In some research, verbal staging has also been used to describe those cases where an offender causes a victim to die in such a way that could appear suicidal or accidental (such as by pushing them from a height), and then initiates contact with authorities to report the death as a suicide or accident (Ferguson & Sutherland, 2018). Similar to missing person verbal staging cases, these homicides may or may not involve manipulation of physical evidence at the crime scene; however, they do involve false reporting to authorities by offenders. Because of the overlap between these behaviors and DA behaviors more broadly (e.g., destroying evidence of the crime), there are numerous examples of cases in the literature that might be described as staged, verbally staged or simply involving DA. As yet, there are blurry lines differentiating the intricacies of these behaviors in the existing definitions. Research on CSS therefore tends to focus on those cases where the definition of staging is more obviously borne out. As discussed by Schlesinger et al. (2012), this is due to the acknowledged importance of understanding and being able to detect CSS in homicide investigations – perhaps even if there exists some ambiguity in its definition.

Despite garnering the most research attention of all DA behaviors, CSS is still an under-researched topic in the criminology literature. Since 2000, less than ten studies have been published on the topic. These studies have been critically summarized elsewhere (see Ferguson, 2015; Pettler, 2016); however, a brief overview of rates of CSS and common victim/offender relationships apparent provides necessary context.

CSS rates

Like DA more broadly, CSS appears to occur in a minority of homicide cases. In a very comprehensive study introduced in Chapter 1, Schlesinger et al. (2012) examined a sample of 946 homicide crime scenes and found 8.4% involved staged evidence ($n = 79$). This is a much greater proportion than that proposed in other research. For example, in Keppel and Weis' (2004) discussion specific to *bodies* being staged, it was found that 0.1% of bodies were staged during one year in Washington State. In 2004, Hazelwood and Napier surveyed 20 experienced law enforcement agents and found these investigators estimated CSS to be present in about 3% of homicides. In an examination of 115 cases, Ferguson (2015) discovered that the rate of CSS may be increasing, a proposal that was first put forth by Geberth (2015) as a further outcrop of the *CSI Effect*. Whether and how the CSI Effect works on offenders to help them learn to use DA and CSS will be discussed in more detail in Chapter 6.

Staging types

There is some disagreement in the literature regarding the type of scene most likely to be staged by an offender. In the first systematic analysis of CSS, Turvey (2000) studied the court documents of 25 staged murders. He found that detected staged scenes were most commonly manipulated to appear as burglaries gone wrong, where the scene was made to appear like an offender broke into a victim's house to steal from them and ended up killing someone. In contrast, Schlesinger et al.'s (2012) study determined that the most common types of staging methods used were arson (25%) and verbal staging (22%), then followed by burglary/robbery/breaking and entering (18%). In arson cases, the staging was presumably meant to imply that the victim(s) died in an accidental fire; while the verbal staging cases involved offenders concealing the homicide and reporting victims missing. As discussed in the first chapter, Schlesinger et al. (2012) noted that staging type differed depending on the relationship between victim and offender, with domestic homicides more frequently involving verbal staging, whereas non-domestic murders more often involved arson.

In Ferguson's (2015) sample, homicides were most often staged as burglaries, followed by suicides, accidents and car accidents. Notably, Ferguson (2015, 2016) is the only author to mention car accidents as a separate type of staging, with others combining car accidents with other staged accidental scenarios, such as those involving firearms or falls. Separating car accidents from other types was rationalized in Ferguson's work since the constellation and number of CSS behaviors differed dramatically between the two (Ferguson, 2015, 2016). That is, staged car accidents involved many more and different behaviors to create the façade than other types of staged accidental death scenarios (Ferguson, 2016).

Hazelwood and Napier's (2004) participants indicated the most common types they have seen were staged burglaries, suicides, accidents, natural deaths and sex crimes. Eke (2007) studied staged and non-staged intimate partner homicides to compare psychological functioning of offenders and found that intimate partners most frequently staged scenes to appear as burglaries, accidents or missing persons (later referred to as *verbal staging*). Important to investigating these homicide scenes, Ferguson (2015) determined that regardless of the numbers of each type of staged scene, they appear to display differently to investigators with separate indicators and common features. Indeed, so different is the presentation of CSS across types that several researchers have proposed typologies to help investigators explain and identify staged scenes and staging offenders. The typologies proposed, and their strengths and limitations are explored in Chapter 3.

Victim and offender relationships in staged cases

Relationships between victims and offenders, or actual homicide type as opposed to staging type, are another important element of CSS research. In such research, the pervading logic is that offenders known to a victim have more reason to stage a scene than those unknown to the victim (Eke, 2007; Ferguson, 2015). To investigate this, most researchers studying CSS have measured victim and offender relationships as a key variable (Ferguson, 2015; Pettler, 2016; Schlesinger et al., 2012; Turvey, 2000), while others have assumed that there would be a relationship between victims and offenders and have thus focused solely on CSS in IPH (Eke, 2007). This assumption is supported in the literature measuring relationship type, with Turvey (2000), Schlesinger et al. (2012), Ferguson (2015) and Pettler (2016) all finding that victims and offenders in staged homicides were almost always known to each other, most often being intimate partners. However, Pettler's (2016) assessment of CSS in North Carolina discovered that a lower proportion of victims and offenders were known to each other (67%) in comparison to that found in Schlesinger et al. (2012; 77%) and in Ferguson (2015; 91%). This can be explained by the broad definition of staging employed by Pettler (2016), as discussed earlier. Recall Pettler (2016) included as staged homicides those that have been defined as involving DA but not staging elsewhere; for example, a homicide where an offender conceals a body without reporting a victim missing.

While including DA behaviors under staging adds a level of difficulty to comparing CSS behaviors specifically, it also helps explain why such low levels of staging are seen in the more general DA literature. As discussed at the beginning of this chapter, the literature on DA in homicides has examined mostly sexual, child and serial murders – crime types where offenders are less likely to be known to or intimate partners of victims and perhaps, then, less likely to involve CSS. Clearly, the mechanism by which some victim and offender relationships influence the use of DA by offenders requires further examination and unpacking. Unfortunately, little research has focused specifically on measuring DA and different types of victim and offender relationships. However, some conclusions can be extrapolated from the research on body disposal by offenders after a homicide, a common type of DA. Both the medical and criminological literature on body disposal further support the important influence of relationships on distance travelled, disposal type and, indeed, whether victims' bodies are ever discovered.

Relationships and body disposal as DA

Intimate partner homicides and DA

In 2007, Häkkänen, Hurme and Liukkonen studied 46 rural homicide cases in Finland where bodies had been disposed but were eventually recovered. They observed (p. 183) that:

> the victim's gender, close relationship with the offender, and the offender's violent crime history were associated with longer homicide-scene-to-body-disposal-site distances.

These findings illustrate two points relevant to the study of DA more broadly: the important role that relationships between victims and offenders play and the impact of criminal experience.

Similar to the general DA literature, most studies of body disposal examine stranger offenders, be they serial or sexual murderers or both. However, there exists some consensus that disposal or destruction of a homicide victim's body may also be associated with an offender's desire to physically distance the victim from their own home or from the offender to obscure the close relationship between them. In her examination of expressive versus instrumental homicides, Salfati (2000) notes that offenders who have a relationship with the victim and/or crime scene often transport and hide the victim's body outside to distance themselves from the crime and to avoid detection. Konopka et al. (2007) add that in many cases, the relationship between victim and offender is the reason behind the use of body disposal, where offenders are aware that they will be a primary suspect if the victim is discovered murdered. Häkkänen et al. (2007) make similar comments, noting that close relationships between victims and offenders, and victims being female, are associated with more effort on the offenders' part to dispose of the victim. Similarly, Preuss et al. (2006) found domestic relationships in all cases of victims being concealed in indoor locations, behind walls or concrete.

In Ferguson and Pooley's (2019b) examination of homicides, where the body was disposed of by the offender and never recovered (referred to as no-body homicides by these authors), a key theme identified was the role of intimate relationships. That is, offenders who murdered their intimate partners were common in this sample, and DA by disposal was qualitatively different in the intimate partner cases than in others. Not surprisingly, the IPH cases in this sample commonly involved male offenders and female victims, or IPF rather than IPH. Offenders did not necessarily have known criminal experience, although some had a long history of reported or unreported domestic violence against the victim and others close to them. Some offenders of this type eventually reported the victim missing to police (verbal staging), and when they did so they often told prescriptive stories about where the victim had supposedly gone. For example, they came prepared to tell authorities that the victim had left with another man or gone on vacation. Not unlike IPF patterns more broadly, witnesses commonly reported that these victims were planning or trying to separate from the offender prior to the homicide. In Chapter 6, more will be said of coercive controlling behavior and the role of DA behaviors in maintaining this control after the homicide.

Serial sexual offending and DA

It is thought that offenders with criminal experience or forensic awareness may be more likely to destroy or dispose of victims' bodies as a countermeasure against detection. This makes sense, since DA behaviors are successful at preventing or delaying arrest, they become more attractive to repeat offenders. Many authors suggest that disposing of a victim's body is indicative of the offender's criminal experience or intelligence, and there is some evidence to support this assertion. For example, in 2004, Kraemer, Lord and Heilbrun found that serial offenders were more likely than single offenders to use multiple crime scene locations and dispose of victims' bodies in remote locations, perhaps due to their level of experience. In their 2007 study of nonfamilial child and female adult abduction homicides, of which 88% were sexual, Häkkänen et al. found that it commonly took days or weeks to locate the bodies of victims, indicating they were transported, concealed or both.

In Ferguson and Pooley's (2019b) no-body cases, along with body disposal, offenders also used other countermeasures to avoid detection. Offenders appeared to be considering DA in the way they planned and executed their selection and approach of victims, often choosing victims who were walking or hitchhiking away from home and alone. Sometimes these victims were thought to have been selected due to being otherwise vulnerable by virtue of being children or sex workers. In some of the no-body cases sampled by Ferguson and Pooley (2019b), offenders had murdered other victims as well, speaking of their level of criminal experience as well as sophistication in concealing previous murders and avoiding apprehension previously.

Criminal enterprise homicides and DA

Homicides involving criminal enterprise, including organized crime or the illicit drug trade, may involve DA in a different way to sexual or intimate partner murders. Literature on body disposal indicates that offenders are commonly intelligent, criminally experienced and/or working in groups, indicating a possible relationship with a criminal enterprise. Ferguson and Pooley's (2019b) results on no-body homicides suggests a similar relationship. They found that, along with permanently disposing of a victim's body, other countermeasures used in these cases included abducting a live victim and bringing them to a remote location, burning the body and/or evidence, cleaning up crime scenes/vehicles and disposing of weapons. Offenders appeared to be criminally sophisticated in cases linked to criminal enterprise and abductions were commonly planned in advance. These findings appear to align with the other body disposal literature, where Häkkänen and Laajasalo (2006) found that drug users were more likely to conceal the victim's body after death than those with less criminal experience. The researchers hypothesized that the criminal histories, and thus criminal sophistication, of drug abusers explained the increased presence of attempted body disposal or concealment. This theory finds some support in Ferguson and Pooley's (2019b) results, where offenders involved in organized crime and the illicit drug trade appear, at least qualitatively, to be more criminally sophisticated than other types of body disposal offenders.

The impact of DA behaviors on death investigations

While there are only a handful of academic studies examining DA in homicides, the research that does exist suggests DA behaviors can be successful for offenders. However, the mechanism under which this works has not been studied and is underdeveloped theoretically. For example, Marche (1994) commented simply that an offender's actions to reduce their risk of being apprehended "obviously" impact whether a homicide can be solved by reducing evidence availability. While the research specific to homicide cases shows this is likely true, how it happens has been the subject of little theorizing. Instead, tangible outcomes of DA on certain types of death and homicide investigations have been described. These findings indicate that DA most commonly works to delay an offender's arrest and prosecution or by complicating investigations. Recently, research has also shown that DA by offenders can create investigative opportunities as much as it creates challenges. Review of this literature leads directly to a proposed framework for the impact of DA on homicide solvability, a discussion of which will make up the remainder of this chapter.

In Salfati and Haratsis' (2001) study of Greek homicides described earlier, it was found that evidence was left and discovered at the scene in many more solved cases than unsolved cases, suggesting the potential value DA has for offenders. Beauregard and Martineau (2014) similarly found that even unsuccessful body disposal as a form of DA delayed recovery, and therefore facilitated crucial evidence being lost or destroyed. This allowed offenders to avoid arrest for a period of time before being apprehended in cases where some part of the victim was eventually found. They note (p. 217) that "some modus operandi behavior adopted by the offender at the crime scene may contribute to delay the discovery of the victim, and thus delay the offender's apprehension".

The extant research shows that even ultimately unsuccessful DA can have alarming impacts on death investigations. In one study, for example, offenders' efforts to have a homicide appear as an accidental fall from a height led to great difficulties for medical and police investigators, with several cases being erroneously classified as non-suspicious deaths for a period of years (Ferguson & Sutherland, 2018). This indicates that the use of DA may prevent the homicide from being deemed such, therefore causing it to remain not only unsolved but also un-investigated as a suspicious death for a significant period of time. Other fall cases involved long and expensive homicide investigations, multiple trials and controversial guilty verdicts (Ferguson & Sutherland, 2018). All of the cases involving these sophisticated DA strategies by offenders appear to be otherwise solvable murders, involving victims and offenders who were known to each other, well-documented motives and many longstanding abusive relationships. Research on falls as a specific type of countermeasure also discovered that there is likely to be a dark figure of similar homicides, which are never discovered or proven to be homicides (Ferguson & Sutherland, 2018). That is, evidence suggests there are cases where fall deaths have been closed as non-suspicious and never discovered to involve criminality – cases where offenders are literally getting away with murder by using DA.

In Australia, countermeasures in the form of disposing of a homicide victim's body create particularly challenging impacts to investigations. The no-body homicide project by Ferguson and Pooley (2019a, b), described earlier, shows these cases commonly involve intimate partner homicides where the offender reports the victim missing, and a homicide investigation may not proceed for sometimes extended periods of time. Such delays, the complexity added by the absence of a victim's body and lies told to investigators and witnesses by the offender result in numerous examples where cases cannot be resolved and perpetrators cannot be prosecuted. Other Australian research shows that the use of fire as a DA strategy to destroy evidence or mutilate bodies postmortem also complicates a homicide investigation. Arson associated homicides similarly often involve intimate relationships between victims and offenders as well as high levels of planning and premeditation. This potentially adds many layers of complexity to the resulting investigation (Ferguson, Doley, Watt, Lyneham, & Payne, 2015).

Studies of homicides staged to appear as suicides show that while usually perpetrated in intimate relationships, these efforts by offenders are often unsophisticated and involve few DA behaviors (Ferguson & Petherick, 2016). Those homicides made to appear as car accidents are also commonly perpetrated by intimate partners, but conversely involve many more elements, such as multiple crime scenes, great efforts to move and position victim's bodies and more DA behaviors being perpetrated (Ferguson, 2016). In Schlesinger et al.'s (2012) examination of levels of CSS in different types of homicides, domestic homicides involved DA at a much higher frequency and higher level of sophistication than sexual or general felony homicides. Even with differences reported in the number or complexity of countermeasures used then, in combination, the literature indicates that DA can prevent or delay homicides being discovered. It shows the simplest DA can greatly confuse a resulting homicide investigation, especially if the victims are otherwise vulnerable.

Ferguson's (2019) examination of DA behaviors perpetrated by offenders with police training (i.e., increased forensic awareness) illustrates some of the most worrying effects of DA on homicide investigations. This project examined the DA behaviors used by 22 offenders who were current or previous police officers when they committed a homicide. Although all cases in the sample were eventually solved and led to an offender being successfully prosecuted, many of the DA behaviors used delayed or complicated the process. Delays to discovering a death or discovering a crime appear to be major impacts of DA in this sample and others. For example, in many cases in the police-trained sample of offenders, the deceased's body and the crime itself were not discovered for many years. This is despite offenders almost always being interviewed by police early in the investigation. The staged burglary, suicide and accident cases in this sample usually involved the police-trained offender claiming that they had discovered the victim and calling police to report the death. In one case the offender was questioned, cleared and 23 years later convicted by a DNA hit.

The staged missing persons and body disposal without staging cases in the police-trained offender study similarly involved delays in the discovery/investigation of the crime, sometimes for long periods of time. In one case the victim's body was never discovered, in another the body was discovered after the offender's conviction on circumstantial evidence and in a third only fragments of the body remained and were recovered. No-body cases in the police-trained sample of offenders led to many added complexities for investigators and prosecutors, including proving that the victim is deceased in the first place as well as proving who the perpetrator is (DiBiase, 2015).

Similar results were shown in Ferguson and Pooley's (2019b) no-body cases. On its own, showing the victim is not alive commonly involves significant delays, meaning the investigation can pass through many hands, witnesses may forget important details and physical evidence may degrade. In cases where bodies are eventually discovered, delays of even a few days can create issues with establishing time, manner and mechanism of death in police and medico-legal investigations (Beauregard & Martineau, 2014).

Even when homicides are solved, it is clear that DA behaviors add other complexities to investigations along with creating delays. In Ferguson's (2019) police-training sample, concealing or setting fire to the victim's body created difficulties for establishing important medical details. Offender's manipulating the body for the purpose of DA in this sample effectively worked to prevent cause and manner of death from being established or made it significantly more difficult to do so. For example, one victim was entombed in concrete; one was wrapped, weighted and dropped at sea; and another was set to light after death. All of these perpetrator efforts obscured evidence of how victims were killed and added complexity to the investigation in the form of expertise and resources required to recover and examine the decedent's body.

DA as an investigative opportunity

Although it is clear that DA can present real and complex challenges to death investigators, once suspicion of the offender is present, DA can also present investigative opportunities. This commonly comes in the form of strengthening circumstantial cases. For example, commentary on one case in the police-training sample included the following description:

> Prosecutors acknowledged from the start that their case was circumstantial. But they pointed to [the offender's] own inconsistent statements as strong evidence that he killed his wife... After the trial, a few jurors also said the inconsistent statements - which [the offender] made to investigators and to [the victim's] relatives – helped prove his guilt... Over the years, investigators conducted 36 searches for his wife's remains and never found anything, which contributed to the delay in taking the case to trial (Dobuzinskis, 2007).

The police-training study also examined other opportunities provided by the use of DA by offenders. To do this, identifying the giveaway to investigators was necessary. That is, what was it that led police investigators to believe the scene was not presenting legitimately or to change a person of interest to a suspect? As indicated above, offenders were questioned as a matter of routine in this sample. Interviews were conducted due to offenders being related or married to victims or being the admitted last person to see them alive. In the qualitative analysis, elements that changed police-trained offenders from being questioned routinely to being questioned as a suspect included things like crime scene evidence not making sense in the staging cases (lack of footprints, point of entry, etc.); subsequent criminal behavior by the offender (one offender's next wife went missing before he was treated as a suspect in the first wife's death); witnesses reporting victims' statements about threats made by the offender; the victim failing to return after supposedly going on a trip; and conflicting information being presented by the offender to police and others, including stories told to police being demonstrably untrue.

The Australian no-body findings by Ferguson and Pooley (2019b) support and expand on these investigative opportunities offered by DA. For example, in the IPH no-body cases, obstacles created by body disposal and other DA behaviors used were overcome, in general, by establishing that an offender's version of events could not comport with the known victimology or evidence available. Offenders giving differing accounts to various parties assisted with establishing the falsity of their statements, as did official and unofficial records of previous IPV by the offender in current or past relationships. Therefore, establishing a suspect's version of events early on appears to present a welcome opportunity for combatting the long-term effects of DA (Ferguson & Pooley, 2019b).

The sexual no-body homicide cases involved the longest time delays in the no-body cases (Ferguson & Pooley, 2019b). Challenges posed by delays were overcome due to the nature of serial sex offences, where trophies or personal effects of the victim were kept by the offenders, and other victims were targeted in a similar way, leading to the availability of propensity, tendency or similar fact evidence (Ferguson & Pooley, 2019b).

Finally, in the criminal enterprise no-body cases, offenders were often known to police and suspected to have a criminal association with the victim (Ferguson & Pooley, 2019b). Offenders were commonly interviewed early after the victim was reported missing. Because multiple offenders were often present in the criminal enterprise cases, they were able to be used against each other by police to garner information. Despite bodies never been recovered in these cases, offenders or co-offenders commonly cooperated with police, admitting their involvement after a period of time and eventually pleading guilty (Ferguson & Pooley, 2019b).

These findings indicate that, depending on the homicide type being investigated, DA can have various tangible impacts on investigations that are both positive and negative. Having acknowledged such effects, the question becomes – can the impacts of DA behaviors on death investigations be prevented? And if so, how? In order to answer these questions, a theoretical explanation for exactly how DA impedes investigations is required as a necessary first step.

DA and homicide solvability – a proposed framework

In order to prevent DA significantly impacting on homicides being solved, a theoretical understanding of how investigations are affected is necessary, in addition to the specifics outlined previously. The mechanisms under which DA can prevent homicides being solved appears to be best explained using the literature on homicide solvability, where several *solvability factors* have been identified. Solvability factors are defined as those pieces of information discovered within the crime event that assist in catching the perpetrator and closing the case (Geberth, 2015). Key solvability factors from the literature include (Geberth, 2015; Mouzos & Muller, 2001):

- Suspect(s) can be identified, even though unknown to the victim/witness
- Suspect(s) is/are known to the victim/witness
- Suspect vehicle can be described and identified
- There is a significant modus operandi, and it fits an established crime pattern
- Knowledge of location of suspect
- Presence of significant physical evidence
- Belief that a crime may be solved with publicity or reasonable additional investigative effort

In addition to these broad factors, Mouzos and Muller (2001) add that when compared to solved homicides, unsolved homicides are more likely to occur in the course of another crime to involve a single victim (as opposed to multiple victims) and to take place in a nonresidential setting. In her analysis of homicide solvability factors in Australia, McKinley (2015) notes that little has changed since these factors were first proposed.

McKinley's PhD research (2015) discovered the process of solving a homicide is extremely complex. In addition to factors previously listed, solvability is directly related to factors like police training, management styles, budget restrictions, conditions of the crime scene and the victims themselves (Geberth, 2015; McKinley, 2015). There are also a multitude of other factors that the police cannot affect in any way, such as bystander interaction, conditions of or at the crime scene (prior to police attendance) and, of course, offender behaviors. These findings suggest the complexity of the relationship that is likely between DA and solvability, where offender behaviors may act to reduce or obscure any number of these factors, leading to the known impacts described in the research reviewed earlier in this chapter.

Given the literature on both DA and solvability, it is clear that the use of DA by offenders has the potential to impact on solvability in a number of ways. Countermeasures like destruction of evidence may delay bodies or evidence being discovered. Concealing a homicide using CSS may confuse manner of death determinations and result in the necessity of a more detailed assessment of whether the death is suspicious. Other types of DA may disrupt links between victims and offenders, confuse the assessment of modus operandi used or limit the utility of witness statements. To begin to explain these complex relationships, the theorized mechanics of how DA behaviors impact on solvability are proposed in Table 2.1. This is done by presenting a framework to link each common DA behavior to several solvability factors it affects. In so doing, a theoretical explanation for how DA by

Table 2.1 Proposed framework explaining effects of DA behavior on solvability factors

	Solvability factors (as per Geberth, 2015; Mouzos & Muller, 2001)								
Detection avoidance behavior (as per Beauregard & Martineau, 2014; Brown & Keppel, 2012; Davies, 1992; Pepper & Salfati, 2008)	**Suspects ID'd; unknown to victim/ witness**	**Suspects known to victim/ witness**	**Suspect vehicle described or ID'd**	**MO fits established crime pattern**	**Witness to the crime**	**Physical evidence present**	**Positive crime scene search**	**Property with characteristics ID'd**	**Belief of solving with publicity or effort**
Destruction or removal of evidence (burning, throwing away, cleaning up/ washing, hiding, cutting up, removing from the scene)	Prevents suspect being ID'd	Obscures relationships between victims and offenders	Vehicle burnt out, damaged or dumped to destroy evidence or link to crime	Obscures MO, complicating pattern association		Evidence removed/ destroyed	Evidence removed from scene	Evidence removed from scene	
Manipulation of the victim's body (disposing of, hiding or covering the body; dismemberment; movement to a different location)	Removes victim from scene associated with offender and victim	Associates body with additional scene				Evidence dynamics becomes problematic	Unknown crime scene if body removed		

Offender protecting their identity (wearing a disguise or mask, wearing gloves, using a condom, moving residence after the crime, giving a false name, changing their appearance)	Suspect harder to ID by witnesses, physical evidence	Suspect harder to ID by witnesses, physical evidence	Stolen vehicle used or plates removed		Suspect not ID-able by witnesses		Red herrings, i.e.: devoting manpower to investigate elements thought to be involved at the expense of other leads, only to learn later elements were unrelated
Acting on the victim or environment (threatening the victim; disabling the lighting, the telephones, security system and/or the victim's vehicle; administrating a drug to the victim; tying up the victim, blocking access in and out of doors or windows; and killing the victim to eliminate the witness)				Obscures MO, complicating pattern association	Obscure surveillance by witnesses, cameras		

(Continued)

Solvability factors (as per Geberth, 2015; Mouzos & Muller, 2001)

Staging the crime scene (manipulating the scene to appear as a different type of homicide, or to impact manner of death determinations, for example, making a homicide appear as a suicide)		Obscures relationships between victims and offenders		Obscures MO, presence of homicide remains controversial		Legitimacy of physical evidence unknown; Destroys or removes physical evidence, time delays	Legitimacy of physical evidence unknown; Destroys or removes physical evidence, time delays		Presence of homicide remains controversial
Verbal staging (reporting the victim missing to police and destroying evidence of the victim's death and the homicide, deliberately causing the victim to have an 'accident' and lying about the circumstances)						Destroys or removes physical evidence, time delays	Destroys or removes physical evidence, time delays		Presence of homicide remains controversial
Using other precautions (securing an alibi, using a look-out, using a scanner to monitor police activities, gagging or covering the victim's eyes)	Suspects alibied out	Suspects alibied out	Suspect actively avoids witnesses		Suspect actively avoids witnesses				

offenders can preclude homicides being solved or complicate their successful investigation is proposed. Common DA behaviors and the solvability factors they affect are taken directly from the research literature described throughout this chapter.

Conclusion

The studies examining DA used in the perpetration of homicide show that behaviors used to thwart investigations are various. Whether, when and which DA behaviors are used runs the gamut depending on the victim and offender relationship and the offender's experience. DA by offenders creates both practical and theoretical challenges to investigations. The cases involving the longest investigations, least physical and most circumstantial evidence appear to be those involving permanent body disposal, which works to obscure links between victims, offenders, crime scenes, vehicles, witnesses and so on. The major impact of DA is summarized well in Beauregard and Martineau's (2014) finding that, for offenders, the most successful way to avoid or preclude detection is by concealing the victim's body to delay discovery. Cases where offenders are very experienced or forensically trained and aware also pose significant challenges. These cases often involve negative searches at suspected crime scene or for bodies, red herrings and difficulties establishing a death has occurred or is suspicious in the first place.

It is also clear that DA by offenders creates opportunities for investigators to fix errors in how deaths or missing people are classified (e.g., erroneously as non-suspicious) as well as creating circumstantial evidence of guilt. Indeed, the most challenging aspect of DA, the resulting time delays, is also the most beneficial aspect, creating an opportunity for offenders to give inconsistent information or allowing witnesses to come forward. Regardless, the complexity added by DA and the increased resources required to investigate homicides involving DA means that these cases require greater examination at both a theoretical and individual level. More research and training are required to identify DA cases early on, to front-load resources to combat these efforts by offenders, to save loved one's years of pain and uncertainty surrounding the victims' death and to prevent homicides remaining unsolved.

The next chapter will explore the research which has theoretically categorized DA behavior, so that it might be better recognized and understood by both academics and investigators. Although such categorizing makes sense intuitively, empirical results reveal lines between behaviors and types of offenders may not be so clear. Chapter 3 therefore critically examines the categorization systems proposed in the research, with an eye toward drawing out as much practical information as possible for death investigators and future researchers.

Note

1 For more details, see research on attrition in sexual assault cases and links with victim-offender relationships and consent, for example, Harris and Grace (1999) and Lievore (2005).

References

Beauregard, E., & Bouchard, M. (2010). Cleaning up your act: Forensic awareness as a detection avoidance strategy. *Journal of Criminal Justice, 38*, 1160–1166. doi: 10.1016/j.jcrimjus.2010.09.004

Beauregard, E., & Martineau, M. (2014). No body, no crime? The role of forensic awareness in avoiding police detection in cases of sexual homicide. *Journal of Criminal Justice, 42*, 213–220. doi: 10.1016/j.jcrimjus.2013.06.007

Brown, K., & Keppel, R. (2012). Child abduction murder: The impact of forensic evidence on solvability. *Journal of Forensic Sciences, 57*(2), 353–353. doi:10.1111/j.1556-4029.2011.01970.x

Chisum, J., & Turvey, B. (2007). A history of crime reconstruction. In J. Chisum & B. Turvey (Eds.), *Crime reconstruction* (pp. 1–35). London, England: Academic Press.

Davies, A. (1992). Rapists' behavior: A three aspect model as a basis for analysis and the identification of serial crime. *Forensic Science International, 55*, 173–194.

DiBiase T. (2015). *No-body homicide cases: A practical guide to investigating, prosecuting, and winning cases when the victim is missing.* Boca Raton, FL: CRC Press.

Dobuzinskis, A. (2007, September 15). Ex-deputy convicted of killing wife will serve 25 years to life. *Los Angeles Daily News.* Retrieved from http://www.dailynews.com/article/ZZ/20070915/NEWS/709159893

Durnal, E. (2010). Crime scene investigation (as seen on TV). *Forensic Science International, 199*, 1–5. doi: 10.1016/j.forsciint.2010.02.015

Eke, A. (2007). *Staging in cases of homicide: Offender, victim and offence characteristics* (Unpublished doctoral dissertation). University of Toronto, Toronto, Canada.

Ferguson, C. (2015). Staged homicides: An examination of common features of faked burglaries, suicides, accidents and car accidents. *Journal of Police and Criminal Psychology*, 30(3), 139–157. doi: 10.1007/s11896-014-9154-1

Ferguson, C. (2016). Collision or collusion? Homicides staged as car accidents. *Journal of Law and Medicine, 24*, 493–503.

Ferguson, C. (2019). Forensically aware offenders and homicide investigations: Challenges, opportunities and impacts. *Australian Journal of Forensic Sciences, 51*(1), 128–131. doi: 10.1080/00450618.2019.1569129.

Ferguson, C., Doley, R., Watt, B., Lyneham, M., & Payne, J. (2015). Arson associated homicide in Australia: a 5-year follow up. *Trends and Issues in Criminology, No. 484.* Canberra: Australian Institute of Criminology.

Ferguson, C., & McKinley, A. (in press). The role of detection avoidance behaviour in solving Australian homicides: A proposed framework. *Salus Journal.*

Ferguson, C., & Petherick, W. (2016). Getting away with murder: An examination of detected homicides staged as suicides. *Homicide Studies, 20*(1), 3–24. doi: 10.1177/1088767914553099

Ferguson, C., & Pooley, K. (2019a). Comparing solved and unsolved no-body homicides in Australia: An exploratory analysis. *Homicide Studies.* doi: 10.1177/10887679198523

Ferguson, C., & Pooley, K. (2019b). Australian no-body homicides: Exploring common features of solved cases. *Journal of Forensic and Legal Medicine.* doi: 10.1016/j.jflm.2019.06.007

Ferguson C., & Sutherland, T. (2018). Murder by pushing: An exploratory analysis of homicidal falls from a height. *American Journal of Forensic Medicine and Pathology.* doi: 10.1097/PAF.0000000000000386

Geberth, V. (2015). *Practical homicide investigation: Tactics, Procedures and Forensic Techniques* (5th ed.). Boca Raton, FL: CRC Press.

Häkkänen, H., Hurme, K., & Liukkonen, M. (2007). Distance patterns and disposal sites in rural area homicides committed in Finland. *Journal of Investigative Psychology and Offender Profiling, 4,* 181–197. doi:10.1002/jip.77

Häkkänen, H., & Laajasalo, T. (2006). Homicide crime scene actions in a Finnish sample of mentally ill offenders. *Homicide Studies, 10,* 33–54. doi:10.1177/1088767905283544.

Harris, J., & Grace, S. (1999). *A question of evidence? Investigating and prosecuting rape in the 1990s.* London: Home Office

Hazelwood, R., & Napier, M. (2004). Crime scene staging and its detection. *International Journal of Offender Therapy and Comparative Criminology, 48,* 744–759. doi: 10.1177/0306624X04268298

Kraemer, G.W., Lord, W.D., & Heilbrun, K. (2004). Comparing single and serial homicide offenses. *Behavioral Science and the Law,* 22(3), 325–43. doi: 10.1002/bsl.581.

Keppel, R., & Weis, J. (2004). The rarity of "unusual" dispositions of victim bodies: Staging and posing. *Journal of Forensic Science, 49,* 1308–1312.

Konopka, T., Strona, M., Bolechała, F., & Kunz, J. (2007). Corpse dismemberment in the material collected by the Department of Forensic Medicine, Cracow, Poland. *Legal Medicine, 9,* 1–13. doi:10.1016/j.legalmed.2006.08.008

Lievore, D. (2005). Prosecutorial decisions in adult sexual assault cases. *Trends and Issues in Criminology, No. 291.* Canberra: Australian Institute of Criminology.

Marche, G. E. (1994). The production of homicide solutions: An empirical analysis. *American Journal of Economics and Sociology, 53,* 385–401. www.jstor.org/stable/3487182

McKinley, A. (2015). *Homicide solvability and applied victimology in New South Wales, 1994–2013* (Unpublished thesis). Bond University, Queensland.

Mouzos, J., & Muller, D. (2001). Solvability factors of homicide in Australia: An exploratory analysis (Vol. 216). *Australian Institute of Criminology.* Retrieved from: https://aic.gov.au/publications/tandi/tandi216

Neimeyer, E., Pepper, K., & Salfati, G. (2008). *Avoiding detection: An examination of adaptive and maladaptive behaviors in serial homicide.* Paper presented at the American Society of Criminology Annual Meeting, St. Louis, MO.

Pettler, L. (2016). *Crime Scene Staging Dynamics in Homicide Cases.* Boca Raton, FL: CRC Press.

Preuss, J., Strehler, M., Dressler, J., Risse, M., Anders, S., & Madea, B. (2006). Dumping after homicide using setting in concrete and/or sealing with bricks—Six case reports. *Forensic Science International,* 159, 55–60. doi:10.1016/j.forsciint.2005.09.010.

Salfati, G. (2000). The nature of expressiveness and instrumentality in homicide: Applications for offender profiling. *Homicide Studies, 4,* 265–293. doi: 10.1177/1088767900004003004.

Salfati, G., & Haratsis, E. (2001). Greek homicide: A behavioral examination of offender crime scene actions. *Homicide Studies,* 5(4), 355–362, doi: 10.1177/1088767901005004006

Schlesinger, L., Gardenier, A., Jarvis, J., & Sheehan-Cook, J. (2012). Crime scene staging in homicide. *Journal of Police and Criminal Psychology, 29,* 44–51. doi: 10.1007/s11896-012-9114-6

Stevens, D. (2008). Forensic science, wrongful convictions and American prosecutor discretion. *The Howard Journal, 47*(1), 31–51. doi: 10.1111/j.1468-2311.2008.00495.x

Turvey, B. (2000). Staged crime scenes: A preliminary study of 25 cases. *Journal of Behavioral Profiling, 1*(3), 1–1.

3 Categorizing detection avoidance behavior using typologies

In order to better understand DA in homicide cases, at least three researchers or teams have proposed typologies to categorize the various behaviors used by offenders or the offenders themselves. Since so little study of DA and CSS has otherwise been done, the development of three typologies demonstrates that the lure of a simple, intuitive system for categorizing offenders or their behavior is very strong. Proponents argue that a typology of DA would provide a useful starting point for researchers and investigators alike, allowing for better empirical study and more efficient and successful investigations. However, an intuitive yet discriminating typology with mutually exclusive types is yet to be found. The three typologies that have been proposed differ in their definition of DA/CSS, their empirical support and their strengths and weaknesses. Each of these typologies is described in this chapter, and overall outcomes of the combination of this literature to explaining DA in homicide is outlined.

As highlighted in the previous chapter, DA can be used by offenders in a variety of ways to hamper investigations. Given enough time and resources, offenders can stage death scenes to look like car accidents, missing persons, suicides, sexual homicides, home invasions and so on. They may also obliterate evidence, delay or preclude bodies being discovered, lie to investigators or utilize any number of other tactics in the hopes of avoiding detection.

To combat these efforts, several researchers and practitioners have noted the importance of classifying DA and CSS specifically, in order to assist investigators and researchers with thinking about and resolving homicide cases involving DA. The most attractive way to do this appears to be by simple classification, using a typology of DA behavior. Indeed, despite the limited discussion of DA and CSS available in the criminology literature, at least three different typologies have been proposed to describe such behavior by offenders. This chapter describes these typologies, including the definitions used, support provided and strengths and weaknesses of each. However, before that, the lure of typologies is described, including the various definitions and terms used for the behaviors and the rationale behind the development of each system.

The lure of typologies

There are (at least) three different proposed typologies to explain DA/CSS behavior. These come from the PhD dissertations of Ferguson (2011) and Pettler (2011) and the experience-based work of Chancellor and Graham (2014). These classification systems are conceptualized here as typologies of DA/CSS because of the various definitions used by each of the authors – some being broader and more inclusive than others. Since the work of each of these authors will be described in detail in this chapter, it is necessary to note the definition each uses to describe the behaviors in their typology as well as the reasons for development of a typology according to them. While each of these authors purports to be proposing a typology for CSS, it is clear that, in fact, two of three are classifying DA behaviors more generally, or are at least including some behaviors that have not been unequivocally defined as CSS or otherwise. Recall from Chapter 2, examples of these ambiguous behaviors might be things like destroying evidence and lying to police, but not reporting the victim missing. So far, the literature has not been unanimous about whether such behaviors would constitute verbal staging or another form of DA. Because of this lack of clarity in the definitions, typologies of CSS might actually describe types of DA in general, including staged and not-staged evidence. Regardless though, the specifics of these typologies, including their definitions, helps illustrate the lure of this type of categorization system for researchers and practitioners.

In 2011, without knowing it, it appears that Ferguson (2011) and Pettler (2011) were simultaneously writing dissertations about CSS in Australia and the USA, respectively. At the time of writing, both authors discuss their work as being the first to study CSS in detail and the first to propose a typology to classify these behaviors. Given the differences in their definitions and findings, neither author is wrong. That is, despite both working with the limited research available on CSS at that time and citing many of the same works, these two authors approached defining and classifying CSS behaviors in very different ways. For example, Ferguson (2011, p. ii) defined CSS as "the deliberate alteration of the physical evidence by the offender to simulate events or offenses that did not occur for the purpose of misleading authorities or redirecting the investigation". The key features of this definition are the *simulation* of events and the goal of redirecting an investigation. Citing Hazelwood and Napier (2004) and Geberth (1996), Pettler (2011) defines CSS as "*any* alteration made to the original state of a homicide crime scene by an offender… Ultimately, the offender's purpose for staging a homicide crime scene is to avoid apprehension for a murder" (emphasis added). While Pettler (2011) stresses the intent behind the behavior being to avoid being caught, the simulation of events requirement seen in other definitions is not included. For this reason, Pettler's work appears to be including other DA behaviors above and beyond CSS, so is therefore best conceptualized as a study of DA rather than staging specifically. Reconceptualizing Pettler's work in this way is in no way a criticism, as the entirety of her writing on the subject is valuable and much needed in the area. Instead, framing the work as a study of DA in general for the purposes of this book transforms it into a practical and comparable addition to the other scant literature available on DA in homicide cases.

The third authors to propose a typology of CSS/DA are Chancellor and Graham (2014). Coming from a law enforcement rather than academic perspective, Chancellor and Graham propose a typology categorizing what they define as staging that may or may not be perpetrated by an offender. Their definition of *primary* staging (committed by the offender and most comparable to other definitions in the literature) states that CSS is:

> An intentional and purposeful, altering or changing of physical evidence or other aspects of the crime scene, and/or providing false information to the police relative to the incident, with specific criminal intent to misdirect or divert a police investigation away from the true facts and circumstances of the crime
>
> (Chancellor & Graham, 2014, p. 21)

Despite criticizing other definitions for being too broad and inclusive, this definition is still very broad in comparison to others in the academic literature. While Chancellor and Graham (2014) include the stipulation that intent must be to misdirect or divert a police investigation, similar to Pettler (2011) they do not go so far as to say that an alternate scenario must be simulated, as done by Chisum and Turvey (2007) and Ferguson (2011, 2015). Like both Ferguson (2011) and Pettler (2011), Chancellor and Graham (2014) do imply that the intent must be to avoid detection. Because of this, Chancellor and Graham's discussion of *primary* staging might also be best conceptualized as one of DA more generally rather than CSS per se.

Differences in definitions aside, Ferguson (2011), Pettler (2011) and Chancellor and Graham (2014) are on the same page when it comes to the necessity and usefulness of a typology for classifying DA behaviors. Ferguson (2011) notes that a typology of CSS is necessary because determining whether a crime has been staged or not is really about determining what the distinguishing characteristics of CSS are, and then being able to recognize them. In more difficult cases, having some empirical basis for making a determination of whether a crime has been staged can therefore be helpful to investigators. Since there are a number of varying scenarios which an offender may intend for the staged scene to resemble, Ferguson (2011) proposes that it is necessary to identify the features of each of those scenarios (types) separately. This can be done by classifying staging behaviors into a typology. Ferguson (2011) adds that typologies have been utilized in the homicide research for decades by several noted scholars, perhaps the most famous being Marvin Wolfgang. Wolfgang (1958) developed a framework for categorizing homicides which set the stage for the use of typologies and classification systems throughout criminology.

Pettler's (2011) rationale for developing a typology of DA is similar but more outcome-focused than Ferguson's (2011). Pettler draws on historical uses of typologies and taxonomies in the study of violent criminals and homicide offenders to argue the necessity of a conceptual model (typology) for identifying DA as early as possible in homicide investigations. She notes (2011, pp. 185–186):

> [DA] is a problem because it depletes valuable resources by misdirecting investigations, hindering the pursuit of justice, and allowing violent offenders to threaten public safety by remaining in society with the opportunity to reoffend... A potential solution to this problem might be to develop a conceptual model of offenders (e.g., taxonomic hierarchal arrangement) coupled with developing an early detection hybrid-methodology to work in tandem to be used by law enforcement professionals and scholar–practitioners that could enable them to utilize resources more efficiently and to remove dangerous offenders from society more quickly.

Chancellor and Graham (2014) have a different take on the usefulness of typologies when it comes to understanding DA behavior. They categorized their version of CSS based on the motive behind the offender's scene alteration – that is, to avoid detection by the offender but not to avoid detection or by someone other than the offender and without criminal purpose. They note that "the benefit of understanding these categories is to recognize that the offender's staging actions can be identified through common findings that are often found when crime scenes are altered" (p. 19). In other words, categories gleaned from examining past cases can help recognize DA in future cases.

Together, these three sets of authors highlight the various reasons why typologies might be useful from both a research and practice standpoint. Certainly, the lure of a typology for streamlining the study and investigation of homicides involving DA is apparent. The next logical question then becomes – can DA or CSS be classified into a typology, and if so, what does such a typology look like?

Proposed typologies

As alluded to at the beginning of this chapter, different researchers from different backgrounds have quite diverse viewpoints about how best to understand and explain DA behaviors. At least three typologies have been used to categorize DA and CSS behaviors. Each has various levels and types of support, and as a result, the associated strengths and weaknesses of each, from both and research and practice standpoint, differ significantly.

Ferguson's (2011) typology

One primary aim of Ferguson's (2011) doctoral research on CSS was to determine empirically whether people staging crimes to look like different scenarios carry out different behaviors at the scene. Put another way, do those whose aim is to make the scene appear as a suicide use different DA behaviors than those who intend for the scene to appear as a home invasion? Although the answer seems obvious, until Ferguson and Pettler's research, there had been no empirical study to determine whether this was, in fact, the case. Several intentions behind staging as well as the common behaviors that go along with them have been identified in the anecdotal literature (Geberth, 2006) and Ferguson's (2011) work tested whether types of staging exist in real cases. In order to conduct this testing, a typology of staging behaviors was proposed that, it was hoped, could be utilized to categorize staging behaviors, to distinguish between them and to study them in more detail.

Ferguson (2011) proposed that an offender may stage a scene with the intention of conveying a variety of differing scenarios. A scene may be manipulated in order to direct attention onto a specific person or group, to conceal the fact that the offender had a previous relationship with the victim, to hide evidence of the crime entirely or it may be used to simulate a crime when none has occurred (although this is extremely difficult in homicide cases). Ferguson (2011) hypothesized that the intentions behind staging behaviors can be broken into seven categories based on the relationship between CSS behaviors and more general deceit explored in the next chapter. These seven categories have been adapted from the writings of Whaley (1982) on how people and animals deceive others in nature. The behaviors proposed by Ferguson (2011) include implicating, mimicking, masking, repackaging, dazzling, decoying and inventing.

1 ***Implicating***: has the purpose of implicating another or directing attention away from the real offender onto another person or group (e.g., making a spousal homicide appear as a mob hit by shooting the victim once in the back of the head, rolling them in carpet and throwing them into a body of water)
2 ***Mimicking***: shows the false scenario by having one thing imitate another; an offender may conceal their relationship to the victim by seeking to mimic another type of relationship through staged elements at the crime scene (e.g., staging a point of entry or exit to mimic a stranger burglary, when, in fact, the offender lived in the home of the victim and had legitimate access to the scene and the victim)
3 ***Masking***: these behaviors hide the real event by making it invisible; this could involve staging behaviors designed to conceal the crime entirely (e.g., cleaning up the crime scene and reporting the victim missing, thus masking the fact that the victim has been murdered and the body hidden)

4 ***Repackaging***: these behaviors are designed to hide the real scenario by disguising it; this could be used to not conceal the death entirely, but to repackage it so that it appears as something which is not criminal at all, such as an accident or suicide (for instance, placing a noose around a strangled victim's neck so it appears they purposely hung themselves)
5 ***Dazzling***: this hides the real events through confusion; these behaviors could involve staging a crime scene in a nonspecific way designed to confuse the nature of the crime thus drawing attention away from themselves (e.g., after a domestic homicide an offender may ransack the home, set the victim on fire as well as position the body and a weapon to indicate suicide)
6 ***Decoying***: these behaviors show the false scenario by diverting attention; this could involve behaviors carried out with the intention of having the homicide appear as though it was justified or excusable (e.g., the offender may injure themselves and place a weapon in the victim's hand in an attempt to make it appear as though they killed the victim in self-defense)
7 ***Inventing***: these behaviors show the false event by displaying another reality which does not exist; this may involve staging efforts designed to simulate a crime when none has occurred, wherein the simulation itself provides the desired end (e.g., those who stage evidence to have it appear as though they were murdered before committing suicide)

Based on the literature available at the time, Ferguson (2011) proposed this typology as exhaustive in terms of explaining the intention of offenders who stage crime scenes. That is, it was proposed that this typology accounted for all of the possible desired results or aims that an offender may have to stage a scene.

After proposing this typology, Ferguson (2011) conducted a detailed statistical analysis of 131 staged homicide cases to see whether different types of staged homicides present with different manifestations of staging behavior. One hundred and one variables, including victim and offender, incident and CSS characteristics, were measured as present or absent across all cases. Multidimensional Scaling (MDS) was then applied and a Smallest Space Analysis (SSA) plot was garnered from the raw data.[1] Ferguson's (2011) results revealed that, despite seven types of CSS being proposed in her typology, only two different types of staging were borne out through the SSA, one of which including two subtypes. While indicating that, as predicted, different types of CSS exist and each involves different specific staging behaviors, this finding also shows that a typology for CSS may not be as intuitive as once thought. The common behaviors carried out in the two different types of CSS that were seen as well as the red flags for those types in Ferguson's (2011) study appear to differ based on whether the scene was staged to resemble a legitimate death or an illegitimate death. Put another way, was CSS used to make the death look non-suspicious (e.g., a suicide, accident or natural death not requiring a homicide investigation) or as a suspicious death of some type other than what it was in reality (e.g., making an intimate partner femicide (IPF) appear as a home invasion burglary/homicide perpetrated by a stranger). While all seven types of staging proposed in the original typology were not borne out statistically, the mimicking and repackaging types fit nicely with the two types seen. Therefore, Ferguson (2011) re-proposed a dichotomous typology instead.

Mimicking illegitimate deaths

According to Ferguson's PhD research (2011), when an offender mimics an illegitimate type of death, they show the false circumstances by having one thing imitate another. An offender may mask or conceal their relationship to the victim by seeking to mimic another type of relationship through staged elements at the crime scene. This can be done by making a non-stranger homicide appear as a stranger homicide by implying through staged elements at the scene that the motivation was sexual or profit oriented.

Based on the statistical analyses performed by Ferguson (2011), this type of staging involves behaviors such as ransacking, a point of entry or exit being staged at the scene, the offender attempting to organize an alibi for him/herself as well as personal items being removed or altered at the scene. A weapon of opportunity was also correlated with this type of CSS, as was the use of a firearm to inflict the fatal injuries, and the offenders injuring themselves in an attempt to lend credence to their narrative. Therefore, the likely red flags that indicate this type of CSS to investigators would involve the removal or disruption of personal items as opposed to those with street value, points of entry or exit which were not actually utilized by offenders or injuries to witnesses/co-victims which may have been self-inflicted. Although some were not particularly common in the sample as a whole, when these behaviors were present, they were most often correlated with staged illegitimate deaths or an attempt to make the relationship between the victim and offender appear as something other than what it was in reality.

Those characteristics which indicate staged illegitimate deaths are also those which may have required greater effort, and perhaps sophistication, than the other types. These more sophisticated behaviors include establishing an alibi and self-injuring. The presence of these behaviors may indicate that deaths which are staged to appear as illegitimate (such as burglaries or home invasions gone wrong) involve some sort of planning on the part of the offender. The relative sophistication element comes into play when one considers that it is not common (in staging literature more broadly) for offenders to try to establish an alibi or self-injure. The fact that these extra efforts are carried out speaks to the experience of the offender, their preparation or their commitment to making the scene believable and avoiding detection.

The second type of staging behavior, which was evident in Ferguson's (2011) analysis, was repackaging designed by offenders to present the death of the victim as a non-suspicious death (i.e., concealed homicides).

Repackaging as legitimate deaths

According to Ferguson's (2011) statistical analysis, repackaging behaviors are designed to hide the real scenario by disguising it. These behaviors are used not to conceal the death entirely, but to repackage it so it appears as something which is not criminal or suspicious at all, such as an accident or suicide. This type could be further broken down into two subtypes involving different scenarios being staged and different types of behaviors by offenders.

Vehicle accidents: The first subtype evident in Ferguson's (2011) study involved behaviors associated with staged car accidents. This subtype included behaviors such as the body being transported and mutilated, a weapon being arranged at the scene, the victim being attacked with blunt force or multiple weapons and being discovered in their own vehicle. The red flags for this type of death, which should be evident to investigators, are evidence that the fatal injuries were incurred at another location (this could be due to a lack of evidence in the vehicle or a presence of evidence somewhere else) as well as mutilation of the body after death and indicators of injuries from multiple weapons (Ferguson, 2011). The car accident scenes in Ferguson's (2011) sample often involved more staging efforts, and therefore perhaps greater sophistication, than other types of scenes. However, they also usually involved CSS elements which were not particularly difficult for investigators to detect (such as the victim apparently dying as a result of a very minor vehicle accident), and therefore these behaviors may not have been well planned. In Ferguson's (2011) staged car accident cases, the offender was more likely to transport the body (which may require planning as corpses can be extremely heavy, awkward and can also increase the chance of detection) as well as mutilation. In some instances, the offender brought accelerants with them to be used in setting the victim/vehicle on fire, and in others the offender brought the vehicle to a location which would facilitate the mutilation, such as a cliff or embankment to roll the car over, thus implying an accident. Examples of these types of behaviors could suggest planning in some instances, but not necessarily. Certainly, they suggest at least moderate sophistication in comparison to the staged accidents and suicides.

Suicide/Non-vehicle accident: The second subtype of repackaging of legitimate deaths involves staged accidents or suicides. In Ferguson's (2011) sample, these cases involved behaviors such as simulating self-injury to the victim, no weapon being used to inflict the fatal injuries (i.e., manual strangulation or beating deaths), the victim being discovered in their own bedroom and the assault happening during or immediately after a confrontation between the victim and offender. The red flags which investigators should be cognizant of in order to identify these scenes, according to Ferguson's (2011) statistical analysis, are evidence of a confrontation or struggle, and no weapon being used on the victim. Those cases involving staged accidents or suicides were perhaps the least planned or sophisticated efforts found in this sample, often only involving the body and weapon being arranged or positioned to facilitate repackaging the scene to appear as a non-suspicious death.

Strengths and limitations of Ferguson's typology

Of Ferguson's (2011) empirically validated typology of CSS, she notes the idea behind categorizing behavior is to be able to determine what the common characteristics of each type are and to differentiate those characteristics from other types. The assumptions inherent in any typology are that the characteristics of each type co-occur within that type, and that the characteristics do not co-occur between the types. The testing of whether there is empirical support for a typology revolves around testing these assumptions (Canter, 2004). The results of testing Ferguson's (2011) original typology show there were no bright lines between the seven staging types proposed, as expected originally. As a result, the new typology was proposed combining several of the similar types into those which are more discrete, while also forging out a new type that was not previously thought to present with a different constellation of behaviors – staged car accidents. In so doing, the assumptions inherent in a typology have been borne out in Ferguson's (2011) analysis, therefore empirically supporting the new dichotomous typology. Indeed, the behaviors that characterize each of the two types happen with some regularity there, and they do not often co-occur between types.

Despite their empirical validation though, the two types found in Ferguson's (2011) work represent very broad categories with quite various circumstances and many possible associated behaviors. The resulting typology is therefore limited by the breadth of the two types, with all staged suspicious and all non-suspicious deaths being grouped together, respectively. The research and practical opportunities offered by these categories are reduced by the fact that the two types of staging found are so broad. As envisaged in the original typology by Ferguson (2011), a more discriminating system would provide greater understanding of CSS behaviors, assisting researchers to progress in a more systematic fashion and assisting practitioners to identify more cases more efficiently.

However, the two categories of staging behaviors that have been identified being easily and reliably differentiated may still help to inform research and case analysis in a number of ways. Most notably, the simple typology proposed makes it clear that different types of literature are applicable to the different types of staging found. Because of this, specific literature can be sought out for reference and to provide context during investigations and research. For example, where wound pattern analysis may be very helpful in a repackaged death (staged legitimate or concealed homicide), it will be less so in a mimicked one (staged illegitimate homicide). Lumping all the DA types together, as has been done in the past in the criminology literature, may not be as empirically useful, as the types involve such different sets of behaviors. Ferguson's (2011) results indicate that researching all types of staged scenes together is mostly an analysis of staged burglaries and suicides, without attention being paid to the intricacies of the behaviors as they exist at the aggregate level, and therefore may not be the best way forward.

While mimicking behaviors (staged illegitimate homicides) present as homicides and will therefore be investigated as such, repackaged deaths (staged legitimate or concealed homicides) involve more esoteric expertise which is usually under the purview of a coroner, death investigator or forensic pathologist. Ferguson (2011) notes that those publishing criminological works have rarely touched on the differences between staged illegitimate deaths versus legitimate ones, despite them involving somewhat different procedures in terms of investigation and potentially very different impacts of DA behavior. In supposedly legitimate deaths, investigators may be at the mercy of medical professionals or coroners who are charged with determining the manner of death, and therefore whether the death should be deemed suspicious and investigated as a homicide (more will be said of policy development to prevent this issue in Chapter 7). Ferguson (2011) is hopeful that with her broad results, investigators may be better able to assist medical experts and coroners with identifying the inconsistencies in the scene or statements of suspects in equivocal cases, thus complementing the medical findings or calling them into question. As noted by Ferguson (2011) and discussed by Saferstein (2004), collaborative efforts between medical personnel, coroners, police and forensic scientists are necessary if what took place prior to, during and subsequent to a sudden death is to be determined. Although involving broad categories, Ferguson's (2011) typology research may provide a starting point for investigators to better assist their collaborators and should allow practitioners of all types to acknowledge that staged suspicious and non-suspicious scenes present differently in the research they undertake. Through better research, collaboration and communication investigators and medical professionals may be able to combine their previously discrete expertise to allow for more informed investigations, prosecutions and literature on the topic of DA and CSS (Ferguson, 2011).

Overall, Ferguson (2011) proposes that her typology, though limited in some ways, can assist researchers working from a purely academic standpoint as well as investigators working pragmatically to decide who the necessary experts are, what behaviors are commonly associated with certain general types of CSS and what red flags need to be looked for in each suspected staged scene.

Pettler's (2011) Typology

Similar to Ferguson (2011), Pettler's (2011) doctoral research examines solved homicide cases involving DA (which Pettler referred to a staging; see discussion at the beginning of this chapter and in Chapter 1) to develop a typology of the types of offenders involved and the behaviors they used to avoid detection. Pettler (2011, p. 72) describes the purpose of her study as:

> To verify the existence of [DA] behaviors of [DA offenders] and to determine if a behavioral pattern existed among them as established by the literature. The verification of the existence of [DA] behaviors is paramount towards the eventual development of a model of the [DA offenders]. Arguably, the purpose of this study aimed to accomplish the first step in this process by establishing typologies of [DA] behaviors upon confirmation of their existence.

Pettler (2011) notes the importance of such a classification system, and indeed research, into DA and CSS more broadly as being twofold. First, DA and CSS appear to be increasing and law enforcement agencies around the world are wasting scarce resources investigating homicides where DA has added layers of complexity. Second, experts seeking to testify in criminal courts regarding DA or CSS have little scientific standards on which to base opinions due to a lack of research in this area. As such, expert opinions are difficult to offer and evaluate, often not reaching the standard required in various criminal jurisdictions internationally. Similar to Ferguson (2011), Pettler argues that even a basic classification system of offenders and their behaviors provides a necessary first step to understanding and explaining homicides involving DA.

Despite having similar goals, Ferguson (2011) and Pettler (2011) approached collecting data on types of CSS and DA in homicide cases quite differently. Unlike Ferguson (2011), who analyzed 141 cases quantitatively in less detail, Pettler (2011) conducted a much more comprehensive analysis of 18 cases using an empirical descriptive content analysis to draw out key themes. Pettler's (2011) data was drawn from homicide case files in the State of North Carolina in the USA. Specifically, Pettler (2011) qualitatively examined full briefs of evidence containing "photographs, law enforcement case summaries, witness statements, defendant statements, laboratory reports, medical examiners' reports, and other court related documents" (p.77). In so doing, Pettler (2011) developed six themes or types of DA offender: the Cleaner, the Concealer, the Creator, the Fabricator, the Inflictor and the Planner. These types were developed both inductively and deductively and were based on the categorization of 93 crime scene behaviors by offenders. The types developed are not mutually exclusive, with some offenders exhibiting more than one type of behavior and some homicides involving offenders who fall into multiple categories.

Definitions of the six types of DA offenders identified by Pettler (2011), their associated crime scene behaviors and relative proportion of cases evidencing that type are as follows (adapted from Pettler, 2011, pp. 161–167):

1 ***The Cleaner***: Evidenced in 10 out of 18 cases examined in Pettler's (2011) sample, the Cleaner attempts to strip the scene of evidence of the crime. The Cleaner attempts to remove traces of blood or other biological evidence with either readily available household chemicals or solvents purchased before or after the crime. The Cleaner might also wash his clothes or the victim's clothing or clean other items affected by the crime (e.g., knives, tools and other weapons). The Cleaner also cleans the method of transportation if a victim's body has been moved (i.e., automobile). The specific behavioral patterns evidenced at these crime scenes include cleaning areas of the scene with cleaning products and using fans or air conditioners to clean the air at the scene.

2 ***The Concealer***: Evidenced in all 18 cases examined, the Concealer secretly places items related to the crime in locations only known to him or her. The Concealer might hide weapons, the body of the victim and other evidence from the crime scene in an attempt to prevent investigators from discovering the truth. The Concealer also conceals evidence by destroying it with the use of fire or water. The Concealer might flee the crime scene or might not report the victim missing. Specifically, concealer offenders may wear gloves or a mask, change clothing of themselves or victims, remove/discard/hide evidence from the crime scene and transport the victim's body.

3 ***The Creator***: Also evidenced in all 18 cases examined, the Creator contributes to the crime scene by moving the victim, moving the weapon or other items to make it appear as though something else happened. The Creator might set up the scene to look like an accident, suicide or sexual assault homicide. If perceptive enough, The Creator might even put blood in locations that does not make sense with the rest of the crime scene. Additionally, The Creator might stage a home invasion by breaking a window, creating tool marks on a door or creating other evidence of forced entry as well. The behavioral patterns evidenced at these crime scenes include behaviors like using a ruse to approach or lure victims, moving victims in the crime scene premortem and postmortem and planting evidence at other locations.

4 ***The Fabricator***: Also seen in every case examined by Pettler (2011), the Fabricator lies to investigators by creating stories such as (a) the victim ran away from his or her children, family, friends and life, (b) the victim committed suicide, (c) the victim was killed in an accident (e.g., drowning), (d) the victim attacked the offender, (e) the victim ran away with an individual of whom he or she was having an extramarital affair and (f) the victim attempted to rob the offender (e.g., pulling a weapon such as a knife or gun). The fabricator might also lie to family and friends

of the victim and/or the offender before or during the investigation. Specifically, these offenders may make contact with police (described elsewhere as verbal staging), give statements to police that are false, claim the death/disappearance is non-suspicious and sell the victim's property/resources.

5 ***The Inflictor***: This category was proposed by Pettler (2011) as involving an offender who wounds him or herself to create evidence of an attack by the victim to pose the theory of self-defense. However, no cases in the sample evidenced the predicted behavioral patterns associated with an inflictor. This category remains in Pettler's typology despite no evidence of it being found in her analysis.

6 ***The Planner***: Evidenced in 9 of the 18 cases examined, the Planner organizes and plans the murder. The Planner might ask to borrow weapons, shovels, vehicles, documents or other necessary tools before actually approaching the victim. Further, Planners bring their own weapons to the crime scene. Planners might also use a lookout during the commission of the crime or stage a vehicle and/or a driver near the crime scene to ensure an escape route. Interestingly, Planners might also plan to kidnap and restrain a live victim and transport the victim to another staged location where the murder and disposal of the body will actually take place (this is reminiscent of the discussion in Chapter 2 regarding criminal enterprise homicides involving body disposal and other DA behaviors). Specific behaviors associated with this type are coming prepared with a helper, restraints getaway or weapon and transporting the victim to another location prior to the murder.

Strengths and limitations of Pettler's typology

There are several strengths and limitations of Pettler's (2011) typology of DA. Key strengths lie in the fact that Pettler's data were made up of complete case files, including a high level of detail. Examining such detailed briefs of evidence means that conclusions drawn in this work have a greater potential to be robust and reliable. Similarly, the systematic examination of full briefs of evidence allowed for a large number of expected variables to be accounted for, and an even larger number of unexpected variables to be developed and assessed qualitatively. In combination, this means the contribution made by this work to the broader literature on DA cannot be understated. Pettler (2011) has added many more common themes and behaviors to the work in existence at the time of her writing, filling a rather large gap in the extant literature at that time. Certainly, such a contribution goes toward meeting the goals outlined by both Pettler (2011) and Ferguson (2011) and allows future research and sudden death investigations to be better informed.

In terms of limitations, perhaps first and foremost is the lack of mutual exclusivity of the categories developed by Pettler (2011). Because there are three types of DA that all offenders exhibit (concealing, creating and fabricating), these behaviors might be better conceptualized as core behaviors involved in DA homicides rather than discrete types. Indeed, in 2016, Pettler noted that (p. 96) "crime scene typologies are not mutually exclusive therefore reducing their application for practical use". Second, due to the small sample size, the sample coming from one small region and the qualitative methodology utilized, generalizability of the results is limited. Given the dearth of research in this area, it is arguable that providing results as detailed as those described in Pettler (2011) is a worthwhile trade-off. However, given the pragmatic aims of the study, and the necessity for more empirical work in the area of DA and CSS described by Pettler (2011), this lack of generalizability is a limitation none the less.

Finally, a broader issue with Pettler's (2011) typology surrounds the issue with how staging was defined, discussed at the beginning of this chapter and in Chapter 1. Indeed, this lack of clarity in the definition has resulted in some ambiguity surrounding whether this work is best described as a typology of CSS or DA more generally. While the latter stance has been taken here, not all would agree with this. Unfortunately, the upshot of this definitional ambiguity is that the application of the typology may be confused by some. Despite recognizing this confusion as a limitation, it also should be highlighted as supporting Pettler's (2011) broader arguments – that much more research is required in the area of DA and CSS to assist practitioners with making decisions about offender behaviors, resourcing and providing expert opinions.

Chancellor and Graham's (2014) typology

Chancellor and Graham (2014) proposed a typology for DA (referred to by them as staging) for all types of crime, not just homicide. Based on their experience as investigators, Chancellor and Graham (2014) argue that there are three types of DA involving various levels of criminal intent and for different purposes. The rationale behind offering a typology, they note, is that investigators can learn from the behaviors of past offenders in order to better understand, identify and investigate others.

Of the three types of staging proposed by Chancellor and Graham (2014), only the first type is relevant to the current discussion. Recall from the beginning of the chapter that these authors referred to this type of DA (or staging) as primary staging for the purpose of avoiding detection. Secondary staging, according to these authors, may be associated with the crime and carried out by the offender, but has a different purpose, such as fantasy. The third type is manipulation of evidence by someone other than the offender and for reasons that do not involve DA (Chancellor & Graham, 2014).

Within primary DA, as it will be referred to here, Chancellor and Graham (2014) identify two subtypes from their experience as investigators. These are *premeditated* DA and *ad hoc* DA. These types are underpinned by anecdotal study rather than empirical research, so a description of method used in their development is not offered. Judging by the authors' backgrounds, presumably the types and subtypes were borne out of years of experience in law enforcement and forensic science in the USA. Case examples are provided as evidence of each subtype and are used to illustrate the differences between the types as well as to allow practitioners to better identify DA of all kinds when it comes across their desks. Indeed, the purpose of Chancellor and Graham's (2014) work appears more solely focused on an investigative assessment of DA or staging. They cite very little empirical research, and all that is cited is similarly law enforcement-focused rather than academic. Likewise, no research or statistical evidence is provided in support of the types identified, and they are presented as factual rather than proposed. The two subtypes of primary DA, Ad hoc and premeditated, are described as follows (adapted from Chancellor & Graham, 2014, pp. 21–29):

1 ***Ad hoc DA***: An intentional attempt by the offender to misdirect police, but without planning or forethought. The key difference between this type and other types is the impulsivity involved in the alteration of the crime scene. Often, these types of scenes involve the removal of evidence more than the addition of it. Such a scene would typically involve efforts by the offender to cover up criminal acts, omissions or negligence by providing an alternate explanation. The changed physical evidence and subsequent statements by the offender is almost always related to self-preservation and a desire to direct attention on to someone else. The offenders' lack of knowledge or inability to remember what exactly happened is a frequent finding in this type of DA because it is easier for the guilty party to maintain the narrative if few details are given. Offenders often paint themselves in the most favorable light, outlining efforts to prevent the incident or their frustration at failing to do so. Offenders report that the incident was out of their power to control or avoid. For those offenders who report being at the scene at the time of the incident, it is not unusual for them to claim a vigorous physical resistance against an unknown attacker, but that they were somehow overpowered or injured and could not resist any further. In this type of DA, because the false narrative is created on the run, inconsistencies are often easy for investigators to recognize and uncover.

   Several examples of ad hoc DA are given by Chancellor and Graham (2014), mostly surrounding accidental homicides where evidence of what truly transpired is removed and statements made to police contain little information but make up the bulk of the DA effort. This type of ad hoc DA does not necessarily involve a death, and an example of this is given as well.

2 ***Premeditated DA***: Premeditated DA may be meticulously planned out ahead of time by the offender. The important characteristic of premeditated scenes is the amount and type of physical evidence that is often provided to establish what is being portrayed. The evidence provided

or the scene alteration is really only limited by the intelligence, imagination and overall life experiences of the offender; however, it might still be basic and unsophisticated. Scenes involving premeditated DA tend to have clear evidence that focuses the police on to the event being portrayed. In these cases, the offender wants the police to have a clear understanding as to what happened, leaving little to no chance the evidence will not be found or will be misinterpreted. It is not unusual in these situations for the offender to be the one that actually points out the evidence to the police to ensure it is found. Evidence in these cases may be exaggerated or too much evidence may be provided, especially if the offender has little experience with the crime type they are attempting to portray. In addition to providing an overabundance of physical evidence, the offender may design a scenario or explanation that attempts to play upon perceived police and societal prejudices and offender stereotyping. Despite this type of DA occurring in various crime types, there are three that are used as themes to misdirect the police investigation more often than others: *interrupted burglary or home invasion, suicide* and *sexual homicides.* Several examples of premeditated DA are given, mostly surrounding false reports of sexual assaults and burglaries with an associated death, both for material gain. Similar to ad hoc DA, according to Chancellor and Graham (2014), this type of DA often does not involve a death, but a false report made to police or other authorities.

Strengths and limitations of Chancellor and Graham's typology

As with the other typologies discussed, Chancellor and Graham's (2014) work presents with both strengths and limitations. First, the typology is broad enough to be quite inclusive of many types of evidence manipulation that investigators are likely to see. This effectively increases the potential applicability of the typology, as it is recognized that investigators might see crime types not involving sudden deaths more often. Such inclusivity in the typology also means that research findings in areas outside homicide can be used to further inform this typology in the future, perhaps increasing its applicability and usefulness even more. Certainly, this wide applicability to frontline investigators is a strength of this typology.

However, there are several limitations present as well. Perhaps most notably, Chancellor and Graham (2014) have cited very little of the research literature available on DA and CSS. While this body of literature is small, ignoring it almost completely means that Chancellor and Graham appear to have started from scratch, repeating some of the mistakes made and limitations found by other authors before them. For example, both Pettler (2011) and Ferguson (2011) proposed typologies that were intuitive and in much the same vein as Chancellor and Graham's (2014). Both Pettler and Ferguson found that despite being based on common sense and the anecdotal literature cited by Chancellor and Graham (2014), neither of these typologies were wholly supported in the analyses conducted. Indeed, both authors commented that the original typologies they proposed, or even the updated versions, require more work to maximize their applicability to practitioners working on the front line of sudden death investigations. By not consulting the work of Pettler (2011) or Ferguson (2011), Chancellor and Graham (2014) may have repeated the error of proposing a common sense-based typology. Indeed, no empirical backing for their typology is offered, meaning that it simply cannot be said whether ad hoc and premeditated types truly appear differently to investigators, involving different associated behavioral patterns and red flags. This is a major limitation in applicability of this typology in both a practical and research sense.

Finally, this typology is also marred by definitional issues. Although framed as a typology explaining CSS, there are no obvious lines between DA and CSS in the behaviors described by this typology; this means that comparison to the broader literature is compromised and possibly application in the field as well. While premeditated DA, described here, appears to be referring to CSS as defined in the criminology literature, this literature is also quick to point out that many CSS behaviors are, in fact, not necessarily premeditated or planned (Ferguson, 2011, 2015; Pettler, 2011, 2016; Schlesinger et al., 2012). Ad hoc DA, described here, appears similar to verbal staging or DA in general, as described elsewhere. However, these behaviors can equally be planned in advance, as indicated in various sources in the criminology literature (Beauregard & Martineau, 2014; Ferguson, 2019; Ferguson & Pooley, 2019; Ferguson & Sutherland, 2018; Pettler, 2011, 2016). The lack of definitional clarity in this typology speaks to the broader issue evident throughout this chapter, book and indeed in the literature on DA and CSS in general – the lack of communication and collaboration between practitioners and academics leading to slowed progress in the understanding and explanation of DA.

Conclusion

This chapter has demonstrated that the lure of a common sense- or experience-based typology to explain DA and CSS behaviors by offenders perpetrating homicides is strong. Several attempts have now been made to explain the DA behaviors of offenders in a way that is both intuitive to investigators and allows for types to be differentiated and easily identified in research. The results of the studies and discussions provided here proves that such an intuitive typology may not be possible to develop, at least at this stage. If it is possible to develop, such a typology may not be as discriminating as might have been envisaged, or the types may not be mutually exclusive. Each of these issues on its own impacts on applicability for practitioners and validity from a research perspective.

Despite the issues with the existing typology research though, progress has been made by carrying out these three research projects. All research presented in this chapter advances the state of knowledge surrounding DA behaviors and indicates that DA may be much more complicated and multifaceted than once suspected (Ferguson & McKinley, in press). The research continues to show that identifying, explaining and understanding DA and CSS is something academics and investigators alike are keen to accomplish, but have so far found difficult to achieve. Perhaps, mostly importantly, it shows that although siloed, everyone working in this area is committed to developing a system to ensure that offenders utilizing DA do not waste valuable social and financial resources of police; that their efforts are identified and resolved quickly; and that the loved ones of victims receive the criminal justice response they deserve.

The next chapter examines DA and CSS from a more theoretical standpoint, as a type of deceit. The deception detection literature is critically reviewed and examined for possible links to detecting DA and CSS in death investigations.

Note

1 For detailed discussion of MDS and SSA, see Ferguson (2011, p. 149).

References

Beauregard, E., & Martineau, M. (2014). No body, no crime? The role of forensic awareness in avoiding police detection in cases of sexual homicide. *Journal of Criminal Justice, 42*, 213–220. doi: 10.1016/j.jcrimjus.2013.06.007

Canter, D. (2004). Offender profiling and investigative psychology. *Journal of Investigative Psychology and Offender Profiling, 1*, 1–15.

Chancellor, A., & Graham, G. (2014). Staged crime scenes: Crime scene clues to suspect misdirection of the investigation. *Investigative Sciences Journal, 6*(1), 19–35.

Chisum, J., & Turvey, B. (2007). Staged crime scenes. In J. Chisum & B. Turvey (Eds.), *Crime Reconstruction* (pp. 441–481). London: Academic Press.

Ferguson, C. (2011). *The defects of the situation: A typology of staged crime scenes* (Unpublished doctoral dissertation). Bond University, Gold Coast, Australia.

Ferguson, C. (2015). Staged homicides: An examination of common features of faked burglaries, suicides, accidents and car accidents. *Journal of Police and Criminal Psychology, 30*(3), 139–157. doi: 10.1007/s11896-014-9154-1

Ferguson, C. (2019). Forensically aware offenders and homicide investigations: Challenges, opportunities and impacts. *Australian Journal of Forensic Sciences, 51*(Supl), 128–131. doi: 10.1080/00450618.2019.1569129

Ferguson, C., & McKinley, A. (in press). The role of detection avoidance behaviour in solving Australian homicides: A proposed framework. *Salus Journal.*

Ferguson, C., & Pooley, K. (2019). Australian no-body homicides: Exploring common features of solved cases. *Journal of Forensic and Legal Medicine, 66*, 70–78. doi: 10.1016/j.jflm.2019.06.007

Ferguson, C., & Sutherland, T. (2018). Murder by pushing: An exploratory analysis of homicidal falls from a height. *American Journal of Forensic Medicine and Pathology*. doi: 10.1097/PAF.0000000000000386

Geberth, V. (1996). *Practical homicide investigation: Tactics, procedures and forensic techniques* (3rd ed.). Boca Raton, FL: CRC Press.

Geberth, V. (2006). *Practical homicide investigation: Tactics, procedures and forensic techniques* (4th ed.). Boca Raton, FL: CRC Press.

Hazelwood, R., & Napier, M. (2004). Crime scene staging and its detection. *International Journal of Offender Therapy and Comparative Criminology, 48*, 744–759.

Pettler, L. (2011). *Crime scene behaviors of crime scene stagers* (Unpublished doctoral dissertation). Capella University, Minneapolis, MN.

Pettler, L. (2016). *Crime scene staging dynamics in homicide cases*. Boca Raton, FL: CRC Press.

Saferstein, R. (2004). *Criminalistics: An Introduction to Forensic Science* (8th ed.). Upper Saddle River, NJ: Pearson Education Inc.

Schlesinger, L., Gardenier, A., Jarvis, J., & Sheehan-Cook, J. (2012). Crime Scene Staging in Homicide. *Journal of Police and Criminal Psychology*, http://dx.doi.org/10.1007/s11896-012-9114-6

Whaley, B. (1982). Toward a general theory of deception. *The Journal of Strategic Studies, 5*, 178–192.

Wolfgang, M. (1958). *Patterns in criminal homicide*. Philadelphia: University of Pennsylvania Press.

4 Uncovering crime scene staging using deception detection

This chapter begins by making a link between DA/CSS and deception more broadly. That is, it is argued that detecting CSS at a death scene might simply be an extension of detecting lies told by a suspect, similar to the work police investigators carry out routinely. Such links are attractive to make, because while there is little research literature available on DA and CSS, a massive body of robust empirical research exists on deception and its detection, spanning more than 50 years. Studies of why people lie, including evolutionary explanations; how they lie; and how these lies can be uncovered abound and are explored here as they relate to CSS. However, this chapter goes on to outline some of the problems with deception detection, including calls to give up the search for a mechanism to detect verbal lies through body language, speech patterns or/and physiological responses. Issues with training police to detect deception and the necessity of using physical and behavioral evidence as well as more traditional cues to deception are explored.

DA in the form of CSS almost always goes hand in hand with offenders lying to police (Eke, 2007; Ferguson, 2015; Pettler, 2015). As outlined in other chapters of this book, sometimes staging by offenders involves deception exclusively in the form of presenting a false narrative to police and using other DA to clean up or destroy evidence of what actually transpired (e.g., see Chapters 1 and 2 discussions of verbal staging). Because of this commonsense link between CSS and deception, some theorists and researchers have considered whether explaining and detecting staging at sudden death scenes is simply a matter of police detecting deception in interviews and at the scene. Although making this link is intuitive, the deception detection literature indicates that training police to uncover concealed homicides using deception detection techniques may not be quite as simple as proponents would like. However, understanding how and why people use deception and how it can be uncovered may still be useful for beginning to unpack and combat the detrimental impacts of CSS on sudden death investigations.

To make the most out of this robust literature for understanding DA and CSS, this chapter will first present the evolutionary motivations for deception and then the possible methods for identifying these behaviors based on the research on detecting deceit. These theories will provide a basis for how lying through the use of DA behaviors is done by offenders, how the real nature of the event is hidden as well as the personal characteristics and evidence necessary for investigators to detect CSS. The characteristics of offenders using DA and CSS, their relationships with victims and the necessary mindset of investigators will be expanded upon in Chapters 5–7.

Crime scene staging as deception

The investigation and recognition of crime scenes which have been staged are, for all intents and purposes, variations of deception detection. When investigating a scene that has been manipulated to present as something it is not, one is unsure whether they are observing the actual evidence of the death as it happened or the evidence of how the offender wished to present the death (Gross, 1924). For the most part then, the investigator observing a sudden death scene is no different from one observing or conversing with a possibly deceptive suspect. They are both responsible for determining whether or not they are being deceived based on the evidence available to them and their interpretation of it. The difference in these two scenarios is that much research has been undertaken on how to tell liars from truth-tellers when it comes to face to face conversations or interviews (e.g., see Bond & DePaulo, 2006; Caso, Gnisci, Vrij, & Mann, 2005; Ekman, 2001; Inbau, Reid, Buckley, & Jayne, 2001; Park, Levine, McCornack, Morrison, & Ferrara, 2002; Porter, Doucette, Woodworth, Earle, & MacNeil, 2008; Stromwall, Granhag & Hartwig, 2004; Vrij, 2000). Unfortunately, as has been discussed in earlier chapters, those investigators seeking to determine the liars from the truth-tellers based on the physical and behavioral evidence left at a crime scene do not have the luxury of this wealth of literature behind them. Compounding this problem, the literature that is available on DA and CSS appears siloed, with high-level academic research uncommonly informing police practice, and practice-focused research somewhat lacking in rigor. The result of this dearth in the literature and siloing is felt most strongly by sudden death investigators. They are at a significant disadvantage when attempting to detect deceit in the form of a staged scene, or even understand it in any detail after it has been detected. It seems possible that since CSS is a physical form of deception and involves verbal deception, perhaps the same theories which apply to traditional deception detection could also apply to identifying CSS. If so, this would go some way to investigators understanding the basics of how to detect CSS, at least. Unsurprisingly though, those theories that address why and how people lie as well as how to detect a liar have their own limitations, some of which are especially relevant to their application to detecting DA in homicides.

Definition of deception

No one is completely honest all the time. Although lying to cover up a homicide is on the more extreme end of the lying spectrum, everyone is guilty of deceiving others at some point, if not regularly. Perhaps the most comprehensive analyses of natural deception come from DePaulo et al. (DePaulo & Bell, 1996; DePaulo & Kashy, 1998; DePaulo, Kashy, Kirkendol, Wyer, & Epstein, 1996; Kashy & DePaulo, 1996). In these works, DePaulo has concluded that lying is a daily event, people lie approximately twice per day or in one-fourth of their interactions with others; people lie less often to those they are emotionally close with (with some exceptions); most people do not feel uncomfortable lying; and for the most part these lies are successful, that is, they are not detected by the person they are directed at or by any observers.

One of the most prolific authors on deception is Aldert Vrij. In his work on detecting lies, he points out (2000, p. 1), "[d]eceiving others is an essential part of everyday social interaction...[w]e try to dupe others more than once each day, and we often try to find out whether others are deceiving us". Deception may be defined as "a false communication that tends to benefit the communicator" (Vrij, 2000, p. 5). In order for something to be classified as a deception, it must also be a deliberate attempt to mislead on the part of the deceiver. Therefore, unknowingly misrepresenting something cannot be classified as lying. As pointed out in Chapters 1 and 3, the same can be said of CSS, where the intent behind the act determines whether or not a scene has been staged. A number of behaviors which could be utilized for other goals can also be considered DA/CSS if the intention behind them is to evade detection or thwart investigative efforts. For example, moving a deceased's body may be done to facilitate medical intervention in some cases, which would not be considered a deceptive action. In cases where the body is moved to have the scene present as something alternate to what it really is, this same behavior would be considered both CSS and deceitful.

Vrij (2000) also notes that lies may be unsuccessful, and they do not necessarily have to be believed or believable in order to constitute deceit. Finally, he explains that you cannot lie to someone who is expecting it. For example, a magician does not lie to his audience as they know that they are observing a trick. Therefore, deception is only present when no forewarning is given to the person being presented with the lie. To summarize then, deception should be defined as "a successful or unsuccessful deliberate attempt, without forewarning, to create in another a belief which the communicator considers to be untrue" (Vrij, 2000, p. 6). This definition falls nicely in line with the notion of CSS, in that staging is an active attempt to create a scenario, or a belief in the investigator, which is untrue and without forewarning, regardless of whether or not it is successful.

Why do people lie?

According to Vrij (2000), there are five different reasons why someone may lie. There are two broad rationales behind lying and the five reasons fall under one of these two rationales. The two rationales include lying for your own benefit (self-oriented lies) or lying to make someone else appear better or for their benefit (other-oriented lies; Vrij, 2000). Those who are deceitful for the sake of others may lie to make others feel better or to avoid hurting a person's feelings. Those who lie for their own benefit may wish to obtain some sort of advantage, for example, getting a better job. They may also wish to make a good impression or to protect themselves from disapproval, or they may deceive others as a way to avoid punishment (Vrij, 2000). It is these self-oriented lies which are of greatest relevance to the current discussion surrounding DA in homicides.

Although it is the case that people lie quite often and for a number of different reasons, the question still remains as to what causes a person to lie. Evolutionary theories provide a useful backdrop for understanding deception in general and CSS specifically.

Evolution and deception

Evolutionary theories maintain that human nature was built from our ancestors' conscious and unconscious efforts to survive and produce viable offspring. At the most basic level, these theories argue that the human condition evolved in a fashion similar to other physical structures because it contributed to our reproductive success. Those capacities which allowed human beings to thrive were naturally selected, while those which were unhelpful eventually faded away. Behaviors were tested throughout generations using trial and error, until those most adaptive were well established and those least helpful disappeared. Since deception assisted in the survival and the reproductive success of the species, natural selection made it a part of human nature. Thus, "we are deceptive animals because of the advantages that dishonesty reaped for our ancestors, and which it continues to secure for us today" (Smith, 2004, p. 12).

Research conducted by Smith (2004, p. 2) reasons, "deceptive creatures have an edge over their competitors in the relentless struggle to survive and reproduce that drives the engine of evolution. As well-honed survival machines, human beings are also naturally deceptive". However, the question which necessarily results from this statement is – *how* does deception assist with survival and reproductive success? To answer this question in as simple a way as possible, examining simple deceptive behaviors of non-human species is helpful.

Deception occurs at every level of life, including in viruses, bacteria, plants, insects, reptiles, mammals and so on. This can be through behaviors such as camouflage, mimicry, posture or avoiding notifying others of the availability of food. In terms of how deceit is used by a species, Trivers writes (2006, p. 374):

> Deception infects all the fundamental relationships in life, parasite and host, predator and prey, plant and animal, male and female, neighbor and neighbor, parent and offspring (including mother and fetus), and

> even the relationship of an organism to itself… Deception can allow you to steal or induce the transfer of food and other resources, engage in extra-pair copulations undetected, manipulate your parents, your mate, your offspring, your neighbors even the maternal (or paternal) half of yourself.

Much more will be said about manipulation of others by offenders in the next two chapters. To answer the question posed above though, deception can be used in numerous ways, by various species to avoid being preyed upon by predators, to gain resources or prevent others from gaining resources as well as to facilitate reproduction with more or higher-quality mates. These functions are significant, as the ability to deceive in order to facilitate them is so important a feature of life that it has altered the entire evolution of species and subspecies of some organisms. For example, if one considers stick insects, it is apparent that deceitful morphology (e.g., convincingly looking like a stick) is so crucial to their survival that otherwise advantageous adaptations were sacrificed to facilitate the trick. These insects evolved to include only one kidney and ovary or testis in order to maintain their appearance. In the trade-off between a better chance of survival and reproduction through a more robust anatomical structure, the ability to avoid predators through deceit won out (Trivers, 2006). This example is not meant to suggest that offenders using DA have unconsciously evolved that way, but simply to demonstrate that the use of deception for gain or self preservation is not only part of the human condition.

In a more relatable and conscious example, recent research has shown that primates also use deception to secretly gather or consume food without exposing the existence of it to their competitors. For example, studies of chimpanzees have shown their ability to gauge whether others can see them approaching food (Hare, Call, & Tomasello, 2006). They then use this information to conceal their food approach strategies from competitors. This is done by chimpanzees both to gain access to more food as well as to prevent access by the competitor (Hare et al., 2006). Hare and colleagues (2006) research shows chimpanzees hide how they are accessing food by approaching it indirectly when a competitor is not watching and by actively concealing their covert approach in order to trick the competitor. That is, they hide their approach, but also cover their attempt to hide! Apparently, the necessity to prevent competitors from securing the food as well as securing it for oneself has led to relatively complex deceptive behaviors developing in these mammals. In this way, chimpanzees are able to access resources before their counterparts, increasing their relative chances of survival.

In terms of human's ability to deceive, it is thought that people differ from other animals in their deceptive abilities, because most nonhuman animals do not intentionally deceive others but use deceptive behaviors only unconsciously (such as through camouflage) (Hare et al., 2006). This would be the case with the above stick insect example, as the insect has no control over its physical appearance. It has been theorized historically that perhaps conscious deceit (such as that involved with deceiving an intimate partner) or lying to manipulate the psychological states of others (such as what a competitor believes to be happening) is strictly a human condition (Cheney & Seyfarth, 1990; Hauser, 1997; Tomasello & Call, 1997). However, the chimpanzee example suggests the notion of conscious deceit being only in the purview of humans is not entirely correct. It seems that higher-order animals may be able to manipulate the perceptions of others through deceit as well.

With the two examples provided above, it is clear the ability to lie has been beneficial to many species, as the chimpanzees accessed more food than their honest counterparts, while the stick insects were less likely to be preyed upon as a result of their deceptive appearance. In many species, including humans, deception can lead to more reproductive success, gaining access to resources or maintaining territory during disputes. While deceptive behaviors were evolutionarily selected on a basic survival level (such as being able to camouflage into our environment to avoid predation), in human societies these behaviors may still meet evolutionary ends by allowing for survival and reproduction in more indirect ways. That is, in a modern human society, lying may not directly lead to food being available (such as with the chimpanzees), but may allow for employment to be maintained, which allows resources to be spent on securing food. It is in this indirect fashion that deceiving investigators in order to avoid detection for a crime may be framed as an evolutionary behavior, where the investigator could be considered a predator. Then, in its most abstract sense, CSS behaviors can be framed as one way that deceptive efforts may manifest. The next obvious question is, in what ways do humans lie?

How do people lie?

In the famous book *Illusion in Nature and Art* (1973), Hinton remarks that people actively distort perceptions for their own benefit. He notes that in nature, deceptions may be purposeful or not (such as a mirage), and those which are purposeful are always to the advantage of the species involved. Similarly, according to Whaley (1982, p. 183):

> Man's deceptions are also either without purpose (unintentional misrepresentations) or purposeful- with intent to deceive. Nature does this unconsciously; man does it either unconsciously (as with self-deception and some deceptions of others) or consciously and, then, always to some perceived advantage.

The advantage alluded to may involve securing resources or mates or avoiding adverse outcomes.

In terms of how lies are perpetrated, there are two functions which may be present. According to Soloman (1920), every deception, whether perpetrated by man or nature, involves elements of dissimulation and simulation. Dissimulation requires hiding what is real, concealing or obscuring the truth from the person or target to be deceived in a covert manner (Soloman, 1920; Whaley, 1982). Whaley (1982, p. 183) explains, "[o]perationally, dissimulation is done by hiding one or more of the characteristics that make up the distinctive pattern of a real thing". In so doing, the truth is covered up, paving the way for a new "truth" to be shown to the target. Simulation is the new perception given to the target, "showing the false" (p. 183). The simulation shows the intended lie by portraying the "distinctive characteristics that comprise the distinctive pattern of a false thing" (Whaley, 1982, p. 183). Recall from Chapter 1, links between DA, CSS, dissimulation and simulation are clear. In the context of a homicide concealed as a suicide, the dissimulation is the act of removing those features from the scene which would be distinctive of a homicide (such as cleaning up signs of a struggle, obscuring signs of a physical fight and so on), while the simulation would involve adding those elements which the offender believes to be distinctive of a suicide (leaving a suicide note, placing a weapon in the victim's grasp and so on).

Whaley (1982) explains there are three different methods of dissimulating a situation or obscuring the truth involved in natural and human deceptions. These are masking, repackaging and dazzling. These behaviors provided the basis for Ferguson's (2011) typology, discussed in Chapter 3. In more detail, according to Whaley (1982, adapted from pp. 183–184).

> *Masking* hides the real by making it invisible. It either interposes a screen, shielding it from the senses (and any intermediating sensors) or the target so it is truly covert, or integrates it with its environment so it is unnoticed, blending into its background, literally overlooked, hiding in plain sight. Operationally, masking is done either by concealing all distinctive characteristics (at least those thought to be available to the target's sensors) or by matching them to surrounding characteristics. This is done in order either to conceal or blend its original pattern.
>
> . . .
>
> *Repackaging* hides the real by disguising. It wraps a thing differently, modifying its appearance. It is simulated metamorphosis. Repackaging is done by adding or subtracting characteristics to transform them into a new pattern that resembles something else.
>
> . . .
>
> *Dazzling* hides the real by confusing. It bewilders, confounds, baffles, perplexes, reducing certainty about the real nature of a thing. Dazzling is done by randomizing or otherwise partially obscuring the characteristics of an object (its precise location, size, color, etc.) or an event (its exact timing, method of operation, etc.) in order to blur their distinctive pattern. Ideally, this modified pattern carries less conviction, conveys less certainty, than the real but underlying one.

Similarly, Whaley (1982) describes three ways in which a situation may be simulated, or by which the façade is shown. These are mimicking, inventing or decoying (adapted from Whaley, 1982, p. 185):

> *Mimicking* shows the false by having one thing imitate another. It duplicates a sufficient number of aspects of the other to give a passable replica. The ideal example is the double (doppelganger). Operationally, mimicking is done by copying one or more of the distinctive characteristics of the thing to be imitated to approximate its distinctive pattern.
>
> ...
>
> *Inventing* shows the false by displaying another reality. Unlike mimicking which imitates an existing thing, inventing creates something entirely new, albeit false. Inventing is done by creating one or more new characteristics to create an entirely new pattern.
>
> ...
>
> *Decoying* shows the false by diverting attention. It offers a distracting, misleading option and is therefore a matter of feints and diversions, literally misdirection. Decoying is done by creating alternative false characteristics that give an additional, second pattern. Ideally, this alternative pattern carries more conviction, conveys more certainty, than the real one.

According to Whaley (1982), in some types of deceptions the methods of dissimulation and simulation are overlapping and nonexclusive. An offender may use any number of these in an attempt to conceal what has actually happened as well as attempt to display something new (see Chapter 3 for a critique of why a lack of mutual exclusivity is problematic in detecting DA). Although not originally designed to explain the behavior of offenders, or more specifically offenders who stage events which never occurred, these categories are useful for explaining the range of behaviors that may or may not be involved at staged scenes. For example, using repackaging, an offender may modify the appearance of a homicide scene making it appear as though the victim has killed themselves or died in an accident. This may be facilitated through the offender removing the firearm from where it originally rested and placing it in the victim's hand. They may also move the victim's body from its original location to a place which is consistent with the façade. Through this behavior, two ends have been met, what actually took place has been hidden and the false scenario implied.

Along with categorizing deceptive behaviors, Whaley (1982, p. 189) also notes that in order for someone to be fooled by the dissimulation and simulation (emphasis in original):

> The target must accept ('buy') the *effect*, perceiving it as an *illusion*. Deception will fail at this point only if the target takes no notice of the presented effect [i.e. staged evidence], notices but judges it irrelevant,

misconstrues its intended meaning, or detects its *method*. Conversely the target will:

- Take notice, if the effect is designed to attract his *attention*
- Find it relevant, if the effect can hold his *interest*
- Form the intended hypothesis about its meaning, if the projected pattern of characteristics is *congruent* with patterns already part of his experience and memory; and or is explained as much by an offender; see Chancellor and Graham (2014) as described in Chapter 3
- Fail to detect the deception, if none of the ever-present characteristics that are *incongruent* are accessible to his sensors

Although probably not done consciously or deliberately, it is the job of the offender to attempt to anticipate these four contingencies and monitor the investigators' responses, while it is the responsibility of the investigator to remain objective and look for incongruities in order to not be fooled. The fact that all four of these elements are necessary to fool investigators highlights the importance of research into how offenders attempt to use them as well as good training and policy that can assist investigators to easily recognize incongruities in the evidence.

Detecting deception

In Whaley's (1982) discussion of dissimulation and simulation, it is noted that these two strategies for deception are never fully achievable, meaning that counter-deception is always possible if investigators have the right tools. The probability of discovering the lie is increased by the deception itself leaving clues. To correctly recognize the presence of these clues to deception and correctly attribute them to a lie, according to Whaley (1982) the investigator needs only the right mindset and process. Whaley (1982, p. 190) explains that detecting the deception is therefore always possible; "the problem is entirely one of technology and procedures and never one of theory" – good news for investigators examining sudden deaths involving DA.

Since it is theoretically possible to uncover an offender's lies, how to detect these when we know them to be present becomes the challenge. In Vrij's discussions of detecting deceit, he theorizes that at certain times lying is more difficult for the liar than others, and as such, sometimes detecting deceit is easier for the detective. The ease with which a lie can be uncovered has to do with the complexity of the lie as well as its consequences. Vrij (2000, p. 11) notes that:

> [L]ying is more difficult when the other person has some form of evidence that a person may well be lying… [l]ying is also more difficult if the other person is suspicious… Finally, a lie is easier to tell when the liar has the opportunity to prepare the lie.

While not often touched on in the deception detection literature, Vrij here highlights an important and relevant aspect of uncovering lies told by offenders or others – the use of evidence.

Traditionally, the literature maintains there are three ways to determine whether or not someone is being deceitful: by analyzing non-verbal behavior, the content of what is said and the potential liars' physiological responses (Vrij, 2000). However, based on the discussion above, and that of other authors (Park et al., 2002; Vrij, 2000), it is also possible that there is a fourth method which may be useful: the interpretation and analysis of any physical evidence which may betray the lie. Through evidence of a person's previous behavior, as opposed to their body language or micro-expressions, their speech patterns and their physiological response, a deceit may be evidenced. As mentioned, this has been mostly overlooked in the deception literature previously, although a few authors have touched on using equivocal evidence to raise suspicion, and then focusing on the first three techniques above. Despite the fact that detecting deception through physical evidence has not been given much attention in the literature, theoretically many of the principles of traditional deception detection seem likely to improve when combined with an examination of evidence at a death scene. One underlying principle of traditional deception detection which may be especially useful for detecting lies in physical evidence is the *motivational impairment effect*.

Since not all lies carry the same consequences, not all liars are motivated to pull off the dishonesty to the same degree. In their study of motivation and detecting deceit, Zuckerman and Driver (1985) determined that the more motivated a liar is to avoid getting caught, the more likely it is their behavior will give their lies away. It is this concept which the three traditional methods of deception detection are based upon (non-verbal cues, speech patterns, and physiological responses). According to Zuckerman and Driver's (1985) research, those with a greater motivation to lie experience stronger emotions (like a fear of being found out), they may think harder than those who are less motivated (because of this fear) and they may try harder to control their behavior. This has been termed the *motivational impairment effect* (DePaulo et al., 1988), and allows for a better indication that the person is lying based on their verbal, nonverbal and physiological responses. The *motivational impairment effect* works in favor of those attempting to detect the deceit, making the lie more obvious on these three measures.

However, it is also possible to expand this motivational impairment to an offender's ability to deceive via manipulating the evidence at a scene. It is possible that those who are thinking harder and trying harder to cover their tracks may experience a very high cognitive load after the crime has taken place, or they may forget their plan if they had one (Beauregard & Martineau, 2014). By being highly motivated to create a façade that did not occur; these individuals may actually leave more evidence of themselves and the real scenario (such as leaving more DNA, footprints, and bloodstains). As explained by Svensson and Wendel (1974, p. 292) and discussed in Chapter 1:

> Even when the murderer has carefully planned the crime and taken all imaginable precautions to avoid leaving traces, they are still found. As a rule, the murderer comes to a sudden realization of the terrible results of his deed after the killing. He may then lose his head completely and try to obliterate the evidence of his act, but in his confused state of mind only works against himself by leaving new clues.

Therefore, knowledge of the *motivational impairment effect* may not just work for detecting deceit in a more traditional fashion but may also allow for detection based on the physical evidence available too. This effect is important to the current discussion because, for the most part, those who stage crime scenes have a lot at stake if the lie is not believed (such as significant time in prison, not receiving insurance pay-outs, losing face, access to children, and reputation) and they may have gone to great lengths to prepare the lie. Together, this pressure increases their motivation to be believed.

Like the determination of deceit in a more traditional sense then, looking for incongruities left at crime scenes may assist investigators in determining whether or not a death scene has been staged. These cues take the form of physical and behavioral evidence instead of things like stuttering, speech rates and so on. Investigators seeking out evidence of paradoxical offender behavior, inconsistencies in the physical evidence and the like are better placed to detect deception by virtue of doing so. Undoubtedly though, these incongruities will be similar to more traditional indications of deceit in that they will become more or less obvious based on the time the offender has to prepare the lie (or staged scene), the consequences and complexity of the lie, and how practiced they are at it (more will be said of deceptive personality types later and in Chapter 5; Vrij, 2000).

Along with the motivation an offender has to be believed, the motivation an investigator has to discover the lie can also have an impact on whether CSS is detected. In terms of the personal characteristics of an investigator necessary to be able to uncover lies, Vrij (2000) remarks that there are several guidelines for investigators to keep in mind. These guidelines are as follows (adapted from Vrij, 2000, pp. 222–225):

> Be suspicious
>
> Lies often remain undetected because observers have too much good faith- too often they assume that people speak the truth. It is essential for a lie detector to be *suspicious* and to distrust what people are saying. This is sometimes difficult.
>
> ...
>
> Be Informed
>
> It is easier for the observer to catch a liar if he or she is *well informed about the topic of the lie.* The more details the observer already knows, the more likely it is that he or she will notice that what the liar is saying is untrue.

> ...
> Watch and Listen Carefully and Abandon Stereotypes
> There is no typical non-verbal behavior that indicates deception, nor do all liars say specific things or avoid saying certain things. It is therefore not useful to make judgments about deceit on the basis of stereotypical beliefs (e.g. 'liars show gaze-aversion', 'liars fidget', 'liars stutter'). Instead, observers should judge each case individually. *To look carefully at how someone is behaving and to listen carefully to what they are saying* is thus essential.

These general guidelines dovetail nicely with the characteristics of a good investigator that have been described in the criminology literature and are canvassed in Chapter 7. Similarities in these two bodies of work illustrate the overlap between detecting deceit and investigating possible criminal behavior. From this it is clear that the theories and principles that surround deception detection can be applied to detecting anomalies in the physical evidence at crime scene, hopefully uncovering CSS. Additionally, a seemingly useful method of deception detection may be to make use of the physical evidence as opposed to, or in addition to, traditional techniques used when interviewing suspects. More will be said of this possibility in the next section "Problems with deception detection", devoted to the problems with traditional deception detection techniques and the need for reform.

Problems with deception detection

In determining how a person detects deception, and how good people are at it, there are a number of useful studies to consult. Most of this literature, with a few exceptions, works on the assumption that people detect lies based on verbal and nonverbal behaviors of the person lying and that those behaviors are different from those of a truth-teller. Although this assumption has recently been challenged, it has traditionally pervaded the research on determining lies from truths.

According to Bond and DePaulo (2006) research on detecting lies has revolved around a premise originally developed by Freud (1905, pp. 77–78), who states "no mortal can keep a secret. If his lips are silent, he chatters with his finger-tips; betrayal oozes out of him at every pore". Freud's notion is utilized in the contemporary empirical research by measuring verbal and nonverbal behaviors that are exhibited by liars, and whether and how other people pick up on these cues. As explained by Park and colleagues (2002, p. 145) most deception detection research therefore includes:

> [O]ne group of participants recruited to serve as message sources. Sources are either instructed or induced to lie, to tell the truth, or both. A different group of participants is recruited to judge the honesty of the sources' messages. Judges are typically exposed to a number of

> messages where half of the messages are true and the other half are lies. Each message is judged for honesty, most often with a dichotomous truth-lie judgment. Accuracy is then calculated as the proportion of correct truth-lie judgments to total judgments.

Results of research such as this reveal that most people have some ability to accurately detect when someone else is lying to them. According to a meta-analysis done by Bond and DePaulo (2006) which summarized the research of 216 studies, people can generally judge deception with about 54% accuracy, significantly better than chance. The accuracy of judgments can be affected by the medium under which the deception takes place, the motivation to lie by the perpetrator, the motivation to detect deceit by the judge, preparation of the lie, previous exposure to the potential liar, the type of interaction that takes place and the expertise of the judge (Bond & DePaulo, 2006). Authors of the meta-analysis found (p. 231):

> Rather than marveling at the outliers in this literature, we are more impressed by the regularity of the results obtained. Despite decades of research effort to maximize the accuracy of deception judgments, detection rates barely budge. Professionals' judgments, interactants' judgments, judgments of high-stakes lies, judgments of unsanctioned lies, judgments made by long term acquaintances - all reveal detection rates within a few points of 50%. We wonder if it is premature to abort the quest for 90% lie detection and accept the conclusion implied by the first 384 research samples – that to people who must judge deception in real time with no special aids, many lies are undetectable.

In no uncertain terms then, people are just not very good at determining whether someone is telling the truth based on the verbal and nonverbal cues of the potential liar. Along with this significant finding, Bond and DePaulo's (2006) meta-analysis also revealed other important results. First, those who are motivated to be believed, regardless of whether they are telling the truth, may appear as liars (Bond & DePaulo, 2006). Second, experts may not be better at determining who is lying from these cues, despite training in the area of deception detection (Bond & DePaulo, 2006). Each of these three issues warrants discussion in more detail as they relate to uncovering concealed homicides and DA.

Generally speaking, people judge lies based on the 'leakage' they expect liars to exhibit because of their reaction to lying. This may include guilt, anxiety and shame (Ekman & Friesen, 1969). According to Stromwall, Granhag and Hartwig (2004, p. 230) "people believe that a liar will feel nervous and act accordingly". People look for cues which indicate these emotions when determining if someone is telling the truth. Many of these inferences, however, may be incorrect (Ekman, 2001). As discussed by Bond and DePaulo (2006), people who are telling the truth and are highly motivated to be believed may also show signs of these emotions, or others which may be mistaken for cues indicating lying. The authors add (Bond & DePaulo, 2006, p. 231):

> Indignant at the prospect of being duped, people project onto the deceptive a host of morally fueled emotions- anxiety, shame and guilt. Drawing on this stereotype to assess others' veracity, people find that the stereotype seldom fits. In underestimating the liar's capacity for self-rationalization, judges' moralistic stereotype has the unintended effect of enabling successful deceit. Because deceptive torment resides primarily in the judge's imagination, many lies are mistaken for truths. When torment is perceived, it is often not a consequence of deception but of a speaker's motivation to be believed. High stakes rarely make people feel guilty about lying; more often, they allow deceit to be easily rationalized. When motivation has an impact, it is on the speaker's fear of being disbelieved, and it matters little whether or not the highly motivated are lying. The impact of motivation is most evident when judges can see the speaker's resemblance to a visual stereotype of the liar.

To put it simply then, those who are highly motivated to be believed may appear as a liar in the verbal and nonverbal cues they exhibit regardless of whether or not they are lying. This is undoubtedly a problem when judging any lie that may be high stakes, when the source is highly motivated to be believed. This high stakes, high motivation scenario is surely present in those instances where someone is suspected of being involved in the death of another person, regardless of whether they behaved criminally.

This brings about the second problem with detecting lies discovered in Bond and DePaulo's (2006) meta-analysis. Because those being questioned may appear as if they are lying even when they are telling the truth, those charged with determining the veracity of their statements are at a disadvantage. It is perhaps because of this problem that experts involved in detecting lies regularly (such as parole boards and police officers) are much more critical of the statements of individuals than nonexperts (Bond & DePaulo, 2006). Experts are more skeptical, and more likely to correctly judge a lie than a regular person. However, they are also more likely to incorrectly judge a truthful statement as a lie than a nonexpert. This may be due to the fact that a higher proportion of the people they are dealing with are highly motivated to be believed, and therefore exhibit the stereotypical cues of deception. As explained by Caso et al. (2005, p. 200):

> Rather than focusing on the differences between liars and truth-tellers, which typically happens in police manuals, the similarities between liars and truth-tellers should be taken into account...Indeed, as our results show, when the stakes get higher, being tense is likely to become

> more dominant. However, truth- tellers will also become more tense, making signs of nervousness less diagnostic than people might expect.

Further compounding the problem is the idea that offenders may be particularly adept at lying. Researchers have theorized that criminals may have more practice lying, they may have better knowledge of what cues indicate deceit, or they may find lying easier than non-offenders based on some aspect of their personality (e.g., psychopaths may find it extremely easy to deceive others; Porter et al., 2008). This issue will be discussed in detail in the next chapter. For now, it is important to note that offenders may not experience the feelings that are typically associated with lying, such as guilt or anxiety, and may even enjoy lying. There is some empirical support for the notion that offenders are better, or at least different when it comes to lying than non-offenders, as noted by Porter and colleagues (2008, p. 36):

> In many ways offenders and non-offenders behave similarly when lying about personal experiences. Notable differences included that offenders smile less and show more self-manipulations during deception. This pattern likely reflects a greater sophistication in offenders' knowledge of how to appear credible.

These findings only take into account those offenders who have been caught though, meaning that captured offenders may have these characteristics when lying, whereas more adept offenders may not. It may also be that those who have evaded capture are even better at lying than their less fortunate offending counterparts, although this would be very difficult to measure. In terms of CSS, the ambiguity of cues indicating deception and truth telling, and the difficulties apparent in dealing with possible skilled liars may mean that determining whether sudden death scenes are legitimate or staged has to hinge on more than the investigator's judgment of the truthfulness of the suspect and their statement. Despite this conclusion, the attraction of training police to use traditional deception detection techniques remains.

Deception detection training

Since it is now well documented that very few investigators are particularly skilled at lie-detection (O'Sullivan & Ekman, 2004) several methods for educating police on how to better detect deceit have been proposed. One of these is Inbau and colleagues' method, which trains officers to recognize specific nonverbal cues to deception (Inbau et al., 2001). Of this training Vrij and colleagues (2006, p. 752) note:

> Whether Inbau's training indeed improves the ability to distinguish between truths and lies remains to be seen. Kassin and Fong (1999) found that participants who were trained to look for the nonverbal cues to

> deception outlined by Inbau et al. (2001) performed significantly worse in a lie detection test that those who received no training. Mann et al. (2004) found a significant but negative correlation between officers reportedly attending to the Inbau et al. cues and accuracy in the lie detection task.

Apparently, training of this type at least, is counterproductive, meaning that scarce resources for educating police officers may be better spent focusing elsewhere. More will be said of this in Chapter 7. However, the absence of deception detection training for officers does not seem to help the situation either. In their study of untrained police officers, Vrij and colleagues (2006) determined that although the officers studied had slightly higher rates of deception detection than those found with lay people in other studies, these rates were not nearly as high as some police maintain. For example, in a study by O'Sullivan and Ekman (2004), no one reached accuracy levels consistently over 80%. The study done by Vrij and colleagues (2006) showed quite positive results, with accuracy rates around 64%. However, despite the fact that these rates are better than what has been found previously, this rate does not inspire much confidence in the judgment of untrained investigators, as they are still making incorrect judgments 36% of the time.

If the training which has been offered does not work, and no training leads to accuracy rates of slightly above chance, perhaps the notion of detecting deception at rates above chance is a lost cause. As discussed in Park and colleagues work (2002, p. 148):

> As active deception researchers, we have sensed a growing dissatisfaction with the state of the deception literature. Authors are beginning to question if nonverbal behaviors are linked to deception. The writer of a recent anonymous review boldly asserted that deception detection research has been "the greatest waste of effort and resources in the history of social science, and was doomed from the beginning," and another reviewer has recently remarked "perhaps we need to stop looking to prior deception literature for illumination about deception processes." Perhaps it is time to question the strongly held assumptions about deception.

In their exploratory study of how people detect deception in real life rather than under experimental conditions, Park and colleagues (2002) have sought to do just that. Instead of assuming that people judge deception based on verbal and nonverbal behaviors, these researchers tested how people know that others are lying to them in real world settings. They found that most people use information from third parties, physical evidence, direct solicited confessions or some combination of discovery methods (Park et al., 2002). Furthermore, they found that (p. 151) "solicited confessions, when they happen, are most often obtained by confronting the liar with third party information, physical evidence or suspicious verbal and nonverbal behaviors". This is particularly relevant to the current discussion as some of the research to date on DA and CSS has indicated that people who confess (and many do) are likely to do so when confronted by inconsistencies which have been recognized in the physical evidence at a death scene (Ferguson & Pooley, 2019; Turvey, 2000).

Park and colleagues' (2002) study, though descriptive and exploratory, indicates that instead of judging lies based on verbal and nonverbal cues, there is a better method which may have accuracy rates higher than slightly above chance. This method of combining physical evidence, witness statements, verbal statements and nonverbal behavior of the suspected liar appears to assist with determining deceit more accurately. Therefore, using such techniques may allow investigators to better judge when they are being lied to by suspects, allowing for better determinations of whether or not DA has been used by offenders at a death scene. This, of course, all hinges on the investigator correctly identifying elements in the scene which may be inconsistent or incongruent with the narrative of the scenario given, and therefore requires them to have the time, resources and skills required to investigate the possibility of deception in the first place.

Conclusion

The theories surrounding how and why people lie allow for a much better understanding of the mechanisms behind DA and its motivations. Unfortunately, though, despite numerous different strategies being available for telling liars from truth-tellers based on verbal, nonverbal and physiological techniques, even seasoned investigators rarely detect lies at levels much above chance. With the addition of advanced training regimes, the rates of correct detection barely fluctuate and, worryingly, sometimes even get worse. Because of this, some researchers have come to the realization that simply talking to a suspect will not be enough to determine whether they are lying or telling the truth (Park et al., 2002). The conclusion must be drawn then that traditional lie detection techniques alone are not the best way to determine if a death scene has been staged or other forms of DA used by offender. Investigators must first have physical indicators which go against the statement of a suspect in order to raise their suspicions, meaning that they must look for signals in the physical evidence or witness statements that may challenge the legitimacy of the evidence presented. Research on the types of people, relationships and behaviors commonly seen in cases involving DA and CSS can be useful for raising these initial suspicions as well as explaining why some offenders choose to use DA and others do not.

The next chapter examines offenders and offense types commonly involving DA in order to begin to explain DA comprehensively. Learning theories, rational choices theories and psychological theories are all explored and their usefulness for informing investigators and researchers alike critiqued.

References

Beauregard, E., & Martineau, M. (2014). No body, no crime? The role of forensic awareness in avoiding police detection in cases of sexual homicide. *Journal of Criminal Justice, 42*, 213–220.

Bond, C., & DePaulo, B. (2006). Accuracy of deception judgments. *Personality and Social Psychology Review, 10*, 214–234.

Caso, L., Gnisci, A., Vrij, A., & Mann, S. (2005). Process underlying deception: An empirical analysis of truth and lies when manipulating the stakes. *Journal of Investigative Psychology and Offender Profiling, 2*, 195–202.

Chancellor, A. & Graham, G. (2014). Staged crime scenes: Crime scene clues to suspect misdirection of the investigation. *Investigative Sciences Journal, 6*(1), 19–35.

Cheney, D., & Seyfarth, R. (1990). *How monkeys see the world: Inside the mind of another species.* Chicago: University of Chicago Press.

DePaulo, B., & Bell, K. (1996). Truth and Investment: Lies are told to those who care. *Journal of Personality and Social Psychology, 70*, 703–716.

DePaulo, B., & Kashy, D. (1998). Everyday lies in close and casual relationships. *Journal of Personality and Social Psychology, 74*, 63–79.

DePaulo, B., Kashy, D., Kirkendol, S., Wyer, M., & Epstein, J. (1996). Lying in everyday life. *Journal of Personality and Social Psychology, 70*, 779–995.

DePaulo, B., Kirkendol, S., Tang, J., & O'Brien, T. (1988). The motivational impairment effect in the communication of deception: Replications and extensions. *Journal of Nonverbal Behavior, 12*, 177–202.

Eke, A. (2001). *Staging in cases of homicide: Offender, victim and offence characteristics* (Unpublished doctoral dissertation). University of Toronto, Toronto, Canada.

Ekman, P. (2001). *Telling lies: Clues to deceit in the marketplace, politics and marriage* (3rd ed.). New York: Norton.

Ekman, P., & Friesen, W. (1969). Nonverbal leakage and clues to deception. *Psychiatry, 32*, 88–105.

Ferguson, C. (2011). *The defects of the situation: An examination of staged crime scenes.* (Unpublished doctoral dissertation). Bond University, Gold Coast Australia.

Ferguson, C. (2015). Staged homicides: An examination of common features of faked burglaries, suicides, accidents and car accidents. *Journal of Police and Criminal Psychology, 30*(3), 139–157. doi: 10.1007/s11896-014-9154-1

Ferguson, C., & Pooley, K. (2019). Australian no-body homicides: Exploring common features of solved cases. *Journal of Forensic and Legal Medicine.* doi: 10.1016/j.jflm.2019.06.007

Freud, S. (1905). *Fragment of an analysis of a case of Hysteria.* Retrieved from: http://icpla.edu/wp-content/uploads/2017/10/Fragment-of-an-Analysis-of-a-Case-of-Hysteria.pdf

Gross, H. (1924). *Criminal investigation.* London: Sweet & Maxwell.

Hare, B., Call, J., & Tomasello, M. (2006). Chimpanzees deceive a human competitor by hiding. *Cognition, 101*, 495–514.

Hauser, M. (1997). Minding the behaviour of deception. In A. Whiten & R. Byrne (Eds.), *Machiavellian IntelligenceII: Extensions and Evaluations* (Vol. Xii, pp. 112–143). Cambridge: Cambridge University Press.

Hinton, H. (1973). Natural deception. In R. Gregory & E. Grombrich (Eds.), *Illusion in nature and art.* New York: Scribner's.

Inbau, F., Reid, J., Buckley, J., & Jayne, B. (2001). *Criminal interrogation and confessions* (4th ed.). Gaithersburg, MD: Aspen Publishing

Kashy, D., & DePaulo, B. (1996). Who lies? *Journal of Personality and Social Psychology, 70,* 1037–1051.

Park, H., Levine, T., McCornack, S., Morrison, K., & Ferrara, M. (2002). How people really detect lies. *Communication Monographs, 69,* 144–157.

Pettler, L. (2015). Crime scene staging: Victim-offender relationship, preceding conflict, victim discovery, verbal staging and murder scene location. *Journal of Cold Case Review, 1*(1), 34–47.

Porter, S., Doucette, N., Woodworth, M., Earle, J., & MacNeil, B. (2008). Half the world knows not how the other half lies: Investigation of verbal and nonverbal signs of deception exhibited by criminal offenders and non-offenders. *Legal and Criminological Psychology, 13,* 27–38.

Smith, D. (2004). *Why we lie: The evolutionary roots of deception and the unconscious mind.* New York: St. Martin's Press.

Soloman, S. (1920). *Strategic camouflage.* London: Murray.

Stromwell, L., Granhag, P., & Hartwig, M. (2004). Practitioner's beliefs about deception. In P. Granhag & L. Stromwell (Eds.), *Deception detection in forensic contexts.* Cambridge: Cambridge University Press.

O'Sullivan, M., & Ekman, P. (2004). The wizards of deception detection. In P.-A. Granhag & L. Strömwall (Eds.), *The detection of deception in forensic contexts* (p. 269–286). Cambridge University Press. https://doi.org/10.1017/CBO9780511490071.012

Svensson, A., & Wendel, O. (1974). *Techniques of crime scene investigation* (2nd ed.) New York: American Elsevier.

Tomasello, M., & Call, J. (1997). *Primate cognition.* New York: Oxford University Press.

Trivers, R. (2006). Deceit and self-deception. In P. Kappeler & J. Silk (Eds.), *Mind the gap: Tracing the origins of human universals.* Heidelberg: Springer.

Turvey, B. (2002). *Criminal profiling: An introduction to behavioural evidence analysis* (2nd ed.). London: Academic Press.

Vrij, A. (2000). *Detecting lies and deceit: The psychology of lying and the implications for professional practice.* Sussex: John Wiley & Sons Ltd.

Vrij, A., Mann, S., Robbins, E., & Robinson, M. (2006). Police officers ability to detect deception in high stakes situations and in repeated lie detection tests. *Applied Cognitive Psychology, 20,* 741–755.

Whaley, B. (1982). Toward a general theory of deception. *The Journal of Strategic Studies, 5,* 178–192.

Zuckerman, M., & Driver, R. (1985). Telling lies: Verbal and nonverbal correlates of deception. In A. W. Siegman & S. Feldstein (Eds.), *Multichannel integrations of nonverbal behaviours* (pp. 129–147). Hillsdale, NJ: Lawrence Erlbaum.

5 Explaining offenders' use of detection avoidance

This chapter explores the theories underpinning the use of DA by offenders in homicide cases. While offenders learning to use DA from the media have been proposed as an explanation, this chapter will discuss that the evidence supporting this theory is mixed. Instead, DA behaviors may be explained using a combination of situational- and individual-level theories. Offenders rationally weighing the costs and benefits of using DA during a homicide and the way they perceive costs and benefits, based on their personal characteristics, are explored. The apparent theoretical and empirical link between DA, rational choice theories and individual characteristics associated with psychopathy are outlined. In sum, it is argued that DA may be a function of several characteristics, including the level of planning before the homicide and the emotional arousal of the offender as two examples.

Presumably, most violent criminal offenders would prefer to evade detection and apprehension; however, only a handful of authors have examined how, why and when DA behaviors are used. This lack of attention creates a significant gap in the knowledge base, where little theory has been proposed to explain DA behaviors (Beauregard & Bouchard, 2010; Beauregard & Martineau, 2014; Davies, 1992; Salfati & Haratsis, 2001). Explanations in the literature commonly include those theories that extend the CSI Effect onto offenders as well as general theories of offending, including Cornish and Clarke's (1986) *Rational Choice Theory*. While such theories may be intuitive, they have yet to undergo direct empirical testing. Links to psychological ill-health have also been proposed as related to the use of DA, but again, have not been tested in detail. In this chapter, the CSI Effect, rational choice theories and/or psychopathy as explanations for whether and which countermeasures are used by homicide offenders are explored. In the next chapter, another potential useful explanation, linking high levels of DA with coercive controlling behaviors in IPF, is proposed.

CSI Effect and DA

It has been demonstrated that offenders are increasingly using DA behaviors, perhaps as a result of popular media publicizing investigative and forensic techniques (Durnal, 2010; Ferguson, 2015; Geberth, 2006; Stevens, 2008). As discussed in Chapter 1, this is seen by some as a further outcrop of the controversial *CSI Effect*, termed the "police chief's version" of the effect by Cole and Diosa-Villa (2007).

Briefly, the *CSI Effect* states that juries' decisions are being skewed by what they have learned through viewing television shows, such as *CSI – Crime Scene Investigation*, which stylizes forensic procedures (Cole & Diosa-Villa, 2007). The "police chief's version" of the effect theorizes that if jurors are learning about forensic techniques through this type of media, then so too might offenders (Cole & Diosa-Villa, 2007). Other researchers have similarly claimed that CSI-type media is educational for offenders, enhancing their awareness of investigative techniques, which results in a change to their modus operandi (MO) with the intent of avoiding detection (Durnal, 2010; Stevens, 2008).

When it comes to the police chief's version of the CSI Effect, the proposed argument has three premises: (1) the more offenders know about criminal investigation from the media, the more forensically aware they become; (2) forensically aware offenders employ techniques to avoid detection; (3) DA efforts are detrimental to investigating and prosecuting crimes.

To test this version of the CSI Effect against other possible explanations, most research has focused on examining the second and third premises of the argument – determining how often DA is employed in various types of criminal samples, which specific behaviors are used by offenders to evade police in different crime types, and whether this affects solvability (Beauregard & Bouchard, 2010; Beauregard & Martineau, 2014; Davies, 1992; Ferguson & McKinley, in press; Salfati & Haratsis, 2001). As discussed in Chapter 2, the small amount of research available has concluded that in most samples, a minority of offenders employ DA, perhaps meaning that few possess forensic awareness. Given the vast range and mass consumption of the genre of procedural media, these findings tend to refute premise one and this version of the CSI Effect – showing that forensic awareness may not be as widespread as the media from which it is assumed to originate (Beauregard & Bouchard, 2010; Beauregard & Martineau, 2014; Brown & Keppel, 2012). That is, if the CSI Effect was working to educate offenders on avoiding detection, higher rates of DA would be expected. Since these high rates are not seen, there may be other or better explanations for why some offenders choose to use DA and others do not.

Rational choice theory and DA

In 1986, Cornish and Clarke proposed the *Rational Choice Theory* to explain criminal behavior. As the name suggests, rational choice theories attribute criminal behavior to reasoning criminals, who weigh rewards and punishments before choosing between different courses of action. Instead of emphasizing the differences between criminals and noncriminals, like other theories, rational choice theories stress some of the similarities, where the same sorts of cognitive strategies are known to be used by criminals and noncriminals when making decisions (Cornish & Clarke, 1986). Rational choice theories are an economic decision-making model, stating that people commit crimes after weighing the costs and benefits associated. In this way, crime can be prevented using deterrence – when the punishment is made more severe. Rational choice theories, situational crime prevention and deterrence gained a significant momentum after 1986; however, by the mid-1990s work on using these theories to prevent and respond to crime dropped off (Tibbetts & Gibson, 2002). Individual-level theories, those taking into consideration characteristics in criminals which are different to noncriminals, came back into favor. More will be said of how individual and situational theories may work together in the next section. For now, findings from the existing literature are used to determine whether or not DA use by offenders may be a rational choice.

Acknowledging that only some offenders use DA, and that they may do so as a result of influences other than from the media, recent research has explained the presence of DA (rather than or in addition to the criminal behavior itself) using rational choice theories (Beauregard & Martineau, 2012, 2014). Canadian researchers have proposed that offenders carry out some DA behaviors but not others due to a cost–benefit analysis involving the specific behavior, the situation and the perceived advantage it would provide (Beauregard & Bouchard, 2010; Beauregard & Martineau, 2014). These researchers do not purport to assume that forensic awareness is coming from anywhere specific, but instead seek to explain how and why some DA strategies are employed in certain cases and not others.

There is modest support for the rational choice model to explain the use of DA. The findings related to CSS outlined in Chapter 2 evidence Beauregard and Martineau's (2014) assertion that choices to engage (or not) in specific DA behaviors are likely to be heavily influenced by the situation in which they occur, most importantly including the relationship between victim and offender. The broader literature adds three important points to the use of rational choice theories to explain DA in homicides. These are: the impact of the offender's perceived risk of being suspected; the risk reduced by virtue of the offender's legitimate access to the victim and crime scene; and the timing of DA behavior and its associated risks in relation to when the homicide occurs.

First, an offender's perception of being suspected by police appears to be an important factor in the choice to engage in DA behaviors (Ferguson, 2018). Those offenders who are otherwise unconnected to the victim may gain little from employing DA behaviors, whereas those who believe they are likely to be suspected may go to extraordinary lengths to avoid being detected and avoid a conviction if they are detected. Eke's (2007) research on crime scene stagers explains an offender's use of staging as a function of the level of association between victim and offender. Pettler (2011) and Geberth

(2006) make similar arguments, noting that countermeasures through staging are most often exhibited by offenders who are associated with the victim and who are seeking to have the homicide appear to have been committed by someone other than the most logical suspect. For example, it is not uncommon for offenders known to victims to initiate an investigation into their loved one's demise as an act of DA (referred to as verbal staging in the literature, see Chapter 1; Ferguson, 2018; Schlesinger, Gardenier, Jarvis, & Sheehan-Cook, 2012). In such a case, an offender may conceal the victim's body and report them missing to police, with the understanding that not reporting their partner missing despite their being absent may present more risk than initiating police contact. Later, and in the next chapter, how and why offenders engage with authorities as an act of DA is explored further.

Second, in cases where victims and offenders are known to one another, the risks associated with carrying out DA behaviors may be lower than for an offender who is a stranger to the victim. Recall from Chapter 2 that risks may be reduced by virtue of known offenders having access to victims in private space and alone, being aware of when others will be concerned about the victim's whereabouts, having legitimate and uninterrupted access to crime scenes in common with the victim, having intimate knowledge of when the victim is at risk and so on. The decreased risk associated with carrying out DA in the homicide of a closely associated victim may therefore impact on cost–benefit comparisons that offenders engage when using rational choices.

Third, although sexual murderers who are strangers to the victim may be more able to employ DA in preparation of the homicide rather than after it (Beauregard & Bouchard, 2010; Beauregard & Martineau, 2014), offenders known to victims appear likely to employ these techniques both before and after the offense. The most elaborate and sophisticated DA behaviors, most often carried out when victims and offenders have close personal or intimate relationships, appear to be commonly planned and executed before and after the homicide (Ferguson, 2018). As indicated, this may be due, in part, to the use of DA behaviors being less risky after the offense for those offenders who have legitimate access to scenes and victims, thus reducing the offender's cognitive load after the offense (Beauregard & Martineau, 2014). Chapter 6 further explores the timing of DA behaviors among different offender-victim relationships; evidently, the offender's perceived increased risk of being a suspect due to their relationship with the victim and determination to kill the victim may also impact on when and how many DA behaviors are employed. Timing of DA as well as whether it is used, then, appear to be at least partly explained by rational choices in the literature available.

To summarize, according to rational choice theories offenders may be aware of forensic procedures, though whether they act on this awareness, to what extent and when will be situationally dependent – occurring at those times and in those situations where the benefit of carrying out the specific

DA behavior outweighs the cost. For example, if an offender believes he will be a suspect in the death of his ex-wife, he may spend extra time and effort cleaning the crime scene, disposing of the body and so on (these efforts are the costs) in order to avoid detection, apprehension or punishment (the benefit). Conversely, in a similar offense when an offender does not believe that they will be suspected – because they have no connection to the victim or crime scene, they are not being monitored by probation and parole or electronically and/or they risk being caught red-handed if they spend additional time at the crime scenes – they may choose not to engage in DA, despite the benefit that doing so could offer.

Though rational choice theories make sense intuitively and some supportive evidence exists, at present the influence of the situation on DA behaviors is not well elucidated from the available literature. Three major critiques exist. First, large sample studies measuring the extent of DA behaviors employed by offenders have not been carried out, making it difficult to explain why offenders have used few strategies to avoid detection in many cases. Second, and perhaps the biggest issue with applying rational choice theories to explaining DA, is the lack of empirical attention given to levels of forensic awareness offenders who use or do not use DA actually possess. In fact, alongside application of the rational choice theory, most of the research seems to suggest that the absence of DA indicates ignorance of forensic techniques rather than a choice not to use DA (Beauregard & Martineau, 2014; Brown & Keppel, 2012). For example, Beauregard and Martineau (2014, p. 218) note that "[serial rapists] do not seem to understand that DNA left at the crime scene can aid in their identification and connect them to the crime scene". However, within this research, levels of forensic awareness possessed by offenders have not been directly measured. In this research, it therefore cannot be said whether offenders are ignorant to the significance of various types of evidence, whether they are unable to act upon the evidence in the circumstances, whether they do not believe the effort to be worth the potential benefit or some combination of these. In reality, those offenders who do not carry out DA may be forensically unaware or, as per rational choice theory, they may choose not to use DA because of the specific circumstances of their position. Therefore, as Beauregard and Martineau (2014) argue – while it seems that employing DA is situational, depending on the perceived costs and benefits of the behavior – the offender's abilities, and their understanding of forensic science are also important factors.

The third major issue with using rational choice theories to explain the use of DA by offenders is that though there is some consensus in the literature that offenders who are forensically aware may choose to employ techniques to avoid detection, exactly how this mechanism does or does not engage is not clear. The situation appears to be an important influence, where offenders may be better able to carry out some behaviors over others depending on the circumstances they are in; however, how this process works has received little attention. More research is required to compare levels of forensic awareness in offenders, the DA they use or do not use and the impact of the specific circumstances of the offending. Further, decision-making processes, situational characteristics and how offenders feel about the homicide need to be examined in more detail before it is possible to say absolutely that DA is simply a result of rational choices made by offenders. In addition to this, individual factors of the specific offender may play a role in how rational choices are made.

Individual factors, rational choices and DA

Does the use of rational choice theories to explain DA mean that individual characteristics of offenders are not as powerful as the situation? Overwhelmingly, the more recent literature on rational choice theories says no. For example, Bernard and Snipes (1996) maintain that in a given situation, individual differences in how people *perceive* expected costs and benefits affect how likely or unlikely they are to engage in criminal behavior. In this way, individual and situational theories do not work separately. Tibbetts and Gibson (2002) explain that rational choices are based on the interaction between the environment and the actor's mind. Supportive empirical literature abounds (Bernard & Snipes, 1996; Jeffery & Zaham, 1993; Paternoster & Simpson, 1996; Piquero & Tibbetts, 1996; Reckless, 1961; Tibbetts & Gibson, 2002). For example, many studies in the mid-1990s showed the interactive effects of individual dispositions and other personal traits and characteristics with rational choices. A study of white-collar offending found that a person's moral beliefs were important inhibitors of crime (Paternoster & Simpson, 1996). When moral inhibitions were high, considerations of the costs and benefits were not important to whether the crime occurred. However, when moral inhibitions were weak, sanctions (costs) had a much greater impact on whether the crime occurred, regardless of whether sanctions were official or unofficial (Paternoster & Simpson, 1996). Therefore, as proposed in much of the recent rational choice theory literature, it is likely that both internal and external factors influence the perpetration of violent crime in the first place, and then potentially the use of DA (Bernard & Snipes, 1996; Jeffery & Zaham, 1993; Paternoster & Simpson, 1996; Piquero & Tibbetts, 1996; Reckless, 1961; Tibbetts & Gibson, 2002). Situation and individual theories likely complement each other to explain the presence or absence of DA, and both perspectives must be considered in order to gain a full understanding of the behavior. One individual theory that appears to have strong links with DA and deception is the role of manipulative personalities or psychopathic characteristics.

Psychopathy

Psychopathic traits are associated with manipulative behaviors and research shows that psychopaths are often adept con artists with long histories of criminality, including frauds and scams (Porter and Woodworth, 2006). Because of the traits of psychopaths and the forethought required in the types of offending common to them, associating DA with psychopathic behavior makes sense. Links between psychopathic traits and rational choices are also well defined, with crimes of psychopaths often involving careful circumspection and instrumental motives (Chase, O'Leary, & Heyman, 2001; Porter & Woodworth, 2006; Woodworth & Porter, 2002). That is, crimes that are rationalized to result in some perceived benefit to the offender (either material or emotional, such as revenge) rather than expressive, hot-blooded actions are more often associated with psychopathic traits and psychopaths than non-psychopaths in the literature on offending (Chase et al., 2001; Porter & Woodworth, 2006; Woodworth & Porter, 2002). As one example, Chase, O'Leary and Heyman (2001) studied spousal abusers and discovered a strong link between psychopathy and the use of instrumental violence in intimate relationships. Out of 60 men studied, 17% of those who perpetrated violence as a means to an end (instrumental) were psychopaths, whereas none of those who used reactive violence were. Indeed, nonviolent and even noncriminal yet harmful behavior of psychopaths is commonly rational, deliberate and premeditated for some material benefit to the offender and at the expense of others (Porter, Doucette, Woodworth, Earle, & MacNeil, 2008).

Moreover, the crimes of psychopaths often involve self-reports of low emotional arousal as opposed to other offenders who report being highly emotional during their offense (Porter & Woodworth, 2006). Such a finding potentially speaks to the cognitive load referred to by Beauregard and Martineau (2014) in their discussion of DA in sexual homicides, with low emotional arousal perhaps being associated with lower cognitive load, at least at certain times during the offending, thus allowing for DA behaviors to be rationalized and perpetrated.

Literature examining murders committed by those with psychopathic traits is scarce, but what is available supports a link between psychopathy and the use of DA. For example, researchers in Canada interviewed 50 murderers, studying their homicide offense and psychiatric history in detail (Porter & Woodworth, 2007). Results showed that those evidencing more psychopathic traits perpetrated more instrumental homicides, but reported to interviewers that the homicide was reactive to something done by the victim. In this way, psychopaths were apt to minimize their role in the offense by blaming the victim and omitting major details from their narrative of the crime. Such attempted manipulation was maintained for long periods of time, often years after the homicide, and continued despite the self-serving version of events being demonstrably untrue (Porter & Woodworth, 2007). Reframing the narrative surrounding murder in such a self-interested fashion is similar to that which is seen by police investigating deaths involving elaborate DA behaviors, where offenders commonly agree to be interviewed and seem to cooperate with police, but maintain their version of innocence for extended periods of time, often in the face of mounting evidence against them (Eke, 2007; Ferguson, 2018).

Psychopathy and deception

If DA is a form of deception (see Chapter 4) linked with rational choices and individual-level factors such as psychopathic behavior, a relationship should exist between psychopathy and rational, deliberate, deceptive behavior. Indeed, such links between psychopathy and deliberate deception are well documented, with lying and manipulative behavior being key features of psychopathy (Hare, 2003). For example, Hare (2003) describes psychopaths as well practiced at lying, with some actively attempting to distract the listener's attention from their deceptions so that they are not detected (Hare, 2003). However, not all psychopaths are equally adept at such characteristic behaviors. Ishikawa and colleagues (2001) compared successful and unsuccessful psychopaths with similarly high levels of criminal offending. They found that successful psychopaths have better capacity for planning, decision-making and greater executive functioning, making them less likely to be caught and convicted of their crimes. Such results speak to particular types of psychopathic traits being better associated with deceptive, rational, DA behavior than others, a finding that is elaborated upon below. Importantly, results reveal that deception by psychopaths is quite difficult to detect, even for police and others well versed in interviewing offenders (Porter & Woodworth, 2007; Seto & Barbaree, 1999). In fact, Seto and Barbaree's (1999) results show just how adept those with psychopathic traits are at deceiving authorities. These researchers studied sex offenders in treatment programs in Canada, finding that those offenders who were rated high in psychopathic traits received the *most* positive evaluations during treatment. These offenders also showed the highest re-offense rates post-treatment, indicating that psychopaths had "put on a good show" during the program through the use of deception (Porter & Woodworth, 2007, p. 94; Seto & Barbaree, 1999).

A relationship clearly exists between rational choice theories and DA as well as among instrumental offending by psychopaths and deceptive, conning and manipulative behavior. The question thus becomes – is there direct evidence of an association between psychopathy and DA behaviors in homicide?

Individual characteristics of DA offenders

Studying CSS in IPH (mostly femicides), Eke (2007) found that offenders who stage crime scenes differ significantly from murderers who did not use DA or who use less elaborate DA behaviors (i.e., not CSS). Differences exist in terms of psychopathic traits, other mental health factors, instrumentality and deliberateness of the offending. Eke's PhD research examines police and mental health files of offenders convicted of murder (or related offences) where CSS was present and compares those files to files matched for time and victim-offender relationship not involving CSS. Cases were compared using several measures, including offenders' Psychopathy Checklist Revised (PCL-R; Hare, 2003) scores; offender and victim biographies; offender criminal and psychiatric histories; relationship characteristics (including risk assessment scores using the Ontario Domestic Assault Risk Assessment (ODARA) tool; Hilton, Harris, & Rice, 2010); as well as offenders' actions at the crime scene and with authorities during the sudden death investigation. The study compared 27 offenders who used DA to stage a crime scene against 27 matched pairs who did not. The purpose of Eke's (2007) study was to develop a screening measure to help identify staging and stagers early on in an investigation as well as to assist with theory building surrounding offenders using elaborate DA behaviors such as CSS. The results of Eke's (2007) work significantly unpack the links among DA, psychopathy and rational choice theories, and are therefore discussed in detail.

DA offenders' psychiatric results

Psychopathy is measured using the PCL-R (Hare, 2003), which examines affect and personality traits of psychopathy (Factor 1), including a lack of empathy for others, a lack of feeling of guilt or remorse and narcissism. The PCL-R also measures antisocial lifestyle characteristics of psychopathy (Factor 2), including as examples criminal versatility, impulsiveness and poor behavioral controls (Hare, 1991).

As suspected, Eke's (2007) research determines that there is a significant statistical link between CSS behaviors and psychopathy. Those offenders who staged death scenes scored higher on Factor 1 (personality) in the PCL-R, with the most common positive results being on items including *lack of remorse or guilt* and a *callous lack of empathy*. This is in contrast to other IPH offenders in Eke's (2007) study, who more often displayed *poor behavioral control* and *impulsivity*. Stagers also scored significantly higher on antisocial, histrionic and narcissistic personality disorder scales than other IPH offenders who did not use CSS. Eke (2007) specifically notes that those offenders who attempted to conceal their partners' death completely by disposing of their partners' body evidenced higher scores on the PCL-R, thus indicating more psychopathic traits.

In terms of other psychopathic characteristics, stagers in Eke's (2007) study were more likely to have elevated levels of conning and manipulative behaviors than non-stagers. As one example, staged cases often involved offenders deliberately manipulating others so that another would "discover" the victim, referred to in previous chapters as *third-party discovery*. Orchestrated victim discovery often involved offenders manipulating neighbors to find the victim with the offender, someone being sent to check on the victim in the offender's absence or offenders setting up the children they shared with the victim to find the body. Given links with increased PCL-R scores and those between DA and deception discussed in the last chapter, it is not surprising that Eke's (2007) stagers were commonly described by health care workers as boastful, storytellers and liars more than other IPH offenders examined in this sample.

Serial offending

If there is an association between psychopathy and DA, it is logical to presume that offenders may have a history of using DA or other types of instrumental manipulation for their own benefit. Such a presumption is borne out in Eke's (2007) findings regarding the history of IPH stagers. Along with higher PCL-R scores and associated manipulative and controlling behaviors in relationships, Eke's (2007) DA offenders also appeared to have long histories of manipulating other people too, including police investigating them. The finding that offenders had faked other events such as fires for insurance, thefts and even deaths of other spouses and family members indicates that for some offenders, manipulative behaviors seen in the staged homicides were a simple extension of other similar behaviors perpetrated previously. As Eke (2007, p. 87) points out, "therefore, the manipulative behavior of these offenders may not be exclusive to murder, rather the staged case of homicide might be an extension of their generally manipulative behavior". The prevalence of offenders using DA to perpetrate other crimes as well as homicide has similarly been discussed in other samples. Ferguson and Sutherland (2018) found a number of cases involving offenders who previously tried to kill the victim or were suspected of killing previous spouses in their sample of fall homicides. Ferguson (2018) found long histories of fraud and deception in her sample of homicides involving DA that were perpetrated by murderers with police training. These histories involved schemes to access insurance proceeds, offenders lying about being CIA operatives, lying about illnesses suffered by themselves or their family and previous spouses who died under suspicious circumstances and from which the offender received financial benefit. This profile of DA offenders as chronically and deliberately conning and manipulative for the sake of personal, financial or emotional gain sits comfortably in the broader literature on psychopathic aggression (Porter & Woodworth, 2006). It also speaks to the reasoning behind the use of DA in homicide or other crime types, where DA appears to be rationally chosen as a mechanism to avoid negative consequences of the offending.

Choosing DA

The instrumentality of psychopathic homicides (Woodworth & Porter, 2002) and the psychiatric results found by Eke (2007) in combination with the versatility of an offender's manipulative behavior speaks to the deliberate rationality of DA, and indeed the homicide that goes with it. The profile emerging is of an offender who has some plan for the homicide, who is likely to gain from it financially, socially or emotionally and who carries out some preparation in anticipation of it, even if only in the offender's head. Such preparation is evidenced in threats to kill the victim commonly seen in other samples as well (Ferguson, 2018; Ferguson & Sutherland, 2018).

Supporting this profile, Eke's (2007) doctoral work reveals that stagers are less likely than non-stagers to misuse alcohol or use substances before the murder, suggesting that offences are more often clearheaded and not reactive. This absence of substance use, especially at the time of the offense, may reflect some offenders' premeditation as well as other offenders' ability to rapidly think about and action an effort to cover up their crime. Such a proposition is supported by Woodworth and Porter's (2002) study of psychopathic murderers, who found that nearly all of the homicides perpetrated by psychopaths (93.3%) were primarily instrumental, meaning they were highly calculated and goal-driven, secondary to the acquisition of an external goal (Bandura, 1983). This was compared to 48.4% of murders perpetrated by non-psychopaths. Similar to Eke's (2007) findings when it came to the use of DA, in Woodworth and Porter's (2002) sample, instrumentality of the homicide was associated with Factor 1 scores on the PCL-R (selfish, callous and remorseless use of others), not with Factor 2 (chronically unstable, antisocial and socially deviant lifestyle).

The deliberateness seen in murders perpetrated by psychopaths is despite these individuals often being characterized by impulsive and explosive behavior (Hare, 2003). Woodworth and Porter (2002) suggest *selective impulsivity* as an explanation, where offenders may choose not to inhibit impulsive aggression when the stakes are low. In instances where an impulsive response is likely to result in severe consequences (such as life imprisonment), psychopaths appear to make very rapid decisions to resist the aggressive behavior or delay their reaction. That is, offenders in these cases are carrying out a rapid costs–benefits analysis similar to that described by rational choice theories. As indicated by Woodworth and Porter (2002), offenders perhaps believe that negative consequences are less likely in planned murders, and thus choose to exact revenge in this fashion rather than in an emotion-laden moment. In this way, for those with psychopathic traits, impulsive aggression is likely to be more controllable than it appears (Woodworth & Porter, 2002). For example, Woodworth and Porter (2002, p. 16) note, "it may be that 'impulsivity' in psychopaths has less to do with a lack of control than with conscious decision making that depends on a rapid consideration of the gravity of the consequences". Findings of such deliberate behaviors among often impulsive offenders support rational choice theories as an explanation for both homicides of this type and the use of DA behaviors within them.

In this group of offenders, the presence of behaviors that appear clear-headed demonstrate that cognitive load may not be present or as powerful as suspected. Cognitive load is suggested by Beauregard and Martineau (2014) to limit an offender's use of DA after a sexual homicide. Cognitive load before and after the homicide may be lowered due to the homicide being orchestrated in advance and/or the psychopathic offender's low emotional arousal, as explained earlier. Eke (2007) also determines that stagers perpetrated their murder and DA when and where there was little chance of being witnessed or caught red-handed, such as in their own home or in remote locations at night. Such situational features could also work to lower cognitive load.

In almost one-quarter of Eke's (2007) staged cases, offenders had professional experience or an interest in law or criminalistics. Such knowledge and experience could also lower the assumed cognitive load and assist in planning the offense. These offenders reported using their law and criminalistics knowledge to help perpetrate the crime, clean it up and create their innocent narrative to report to police. Eke (2007) refers to one example where an offender learned that sometimes people "just disappear", and sought to use this lesson to inform his mental script for the disappearance of his victim.

Also speaking toward the deliberateness and instrumentality that appears to underpin DA, Eke (2007) finds that overkill behaviors were less likely in the cases involving staging than in other IPH cases examined. Generally, the presence of overkill is assumed to indicate anger, rage and emotional arousal by the offender. Instead of this being present, staged homicides in Eke's sample were more likely to involve manual strangulation, drowning and decapitation. These causes of death take time to perpetrate, and help facilitate manipulating the manner of death presentation or complicate identifying the victim's body. Interestingly, in their examination of psychopathic sexual murders, Porter, Woodworth, Earle, Drugge and Boer (2003) find greater use of gratuitous violence, including torture, beating and multiple weapons, and sadistic violence where it was evident that pleasure was derived from inflicting violence. However, the authors reason that these findings were evidence of psychopaths taking pleasure from the suffering of others more than being related to the emotional arousal associated with overkill.

Importantly, two offenders in Eke's (2007) sample also self-injured in an attempt to corroborate their story surrounding the death of their partners. Such a behavior, even when the injury is minor, requires significant commitment and fortitude by the offender, speaking to a concerted effort involved in the staging. Similar self-injury behaviors have been observed in other DA samples, with Ferguson (2015) finding self-injury in 19% of cases where offenders claim that the death was the result of an intruder. In general, self-directed aggression by psychopaths occurs often, is highly instrumental and rarely lethal (Porter & Woodworth, 2006). Porter and Woodworth (2006) indicate that psychopaths engage in self-harm commonly but insincerely. These attempts are designed exclusively to manipulate others, a finding which is consistent with the results of the DA literature involving self-harm. Moreover, Cleckley (1976) notes that psychopaths rarely commit suicide, though they frequently make threats of self-harm and engage in dramatic attempts, which are often premediated and manipulative by design.

Offenders' engaging with authorities

Exemplifying the role of a manipulative personality in evading detection for a homicide is the extent to which offenders using DA "assist" police during the homicide investigation. Of course, if using CSS to direct suspicion away from themselves and/or onto someone else, interacting with the police is necessary to maintain a perception of innocence. The willingness and even eagerness of DA offenders to engage with police appears in contrast to other types of homicide offenders who are likely to avoid police or flee. Eke's (2007) work reveals that stagers are more likely than non-stagers to make themselves available for a police interview immediately on contact by authorities. While some offenders attempted to delay authorities from being contacted, these offenders nonetheless all cooperated immediately once police were involved. Like those seen in other samples, offenders in Eke's (2007) sample often attempted to assist police by offering up possible explanations for the death and/or suspects to follow up on. These findings are consistent with work by Ferguson (2018), who notes that offenders with police training commonly attempted to secure an alibi for the time the victim was murdered, or otherwise attempted to derail the death investigation while appearing helpful. Several offenders in Ferguson's (2018) sample were able to manipulate loved ones by convincing them to corroborate their alibi. Together with recruiting a helper to discover the victim's body, these efforts are used to legitimize the story told by the offender, where at least certain details can be corroborated (Ferguson, 2018).

Importantly, Eke's (2007) comparative study measured impressions of first responders at death or missing persons' scenes, and found that suspicions of the offender were often noted right from the outset. This finding shows that, though offenders may be skilled manipulators, to stranger first responders such personalities and the related tampering of evidence at the crime scene were relatively transparent. It should be noted however that all offenders in this sample were eventually detected and then convicted, meaning that more adept offenders may not be so obvious to first responders (i.e., recall Ishikawa et al.'s (2001) work comparing successful and unsuccessful criminal psychopaths).

Finally, there is also evidence to suggest that along with manipulating others as a matter of routine, DA offenders also attempt to influence the criminal justice process. Much more is said of this in the next chapter, though here it is important to note that stagers in Eke's sample were less likely to confess to the homicide despite strong evidence against them. Those who refused to confess also showed significantly higher PCL-R scores, suggesting a link between psychopathic traits and persistence of the instrumental motives behind the offending and DA. These offenders demonstrated a refusal to take responsibility for their actions and rigidity in externalizing blame for the homicide, perhaps related to the anticipated outcome of continuing to use DA to maintain their innocence (Eke, 2007). The murderers who did confess were significantly less likely to be found guilty of first-degree murder, suggesting real benefits to confessing, which may be unknown by or unattractive to offenders with high PCL-R scores. Other samples examining DA and CSS observe a refusal to confess and rigidity in maintaining the innocent scenario, especially in those cases where the offender is convicted in absence of the victim's body (Ferguson & Pooley, 2019).

Conclusion

In 2006, Porter and Woodworth studied the behavior of psychopaths and found that the types of offences psychopaths choose to commit are related to their psychopathic personality traits. Psychopaths choose to commit crimes for instrumental reasons and do so using manipulation and deceit. In this way, the rational choice to use DA during a homicide can be explained as another example of many manipulative and self-serving behaviors. Indeed, there appears to be both a theoretical and empirical link between DA, rational choice theories and individual characteristics associated with psychopathy. Moreover, characteristics such as lack of remorse, manipulativeness and failure to accept responsibility are documented in both homicides involving DA (Eke, 2007) as well as IPH more broadly (Monckton Smith, 2019), where the link with DA is also strong (Ferguson, 2015; Schlesinger et al., 2012).

This chapter set out to explore the theories underpinning the use of DA in homicide cases. While evidence of offenders learning to use DA from the media is mixed, strong evidence exists that regardless of where it is learned, DA behaviors can be explained using a combination of situational- and individual-level theories. Although offenders appear to rationally weigh the costs and benefits of using DA during a homicide, the way they perceive costs and benefits is likely to be impacted by their personal characteristics. DA may be a function of several characteristics, including the level of planning before the homicide and the emotional arousal of the offender as examples.

In the next chapter, the characteristics of relationships that end in IPF are examined to further unpack the potential role of individual factors in explaining when and why some offenders choose to use DA in their perpetration of a homicide.

References

Bandura, A. (1983). Psychological mechanisms of aggression. In R. G. Green & E. I. Donnerstein (Eds.), *Aggression: Theoretical and empirical views* (Vol. 1, pp. 1–40). New York: Academic Press.

Beauregard, E., & Bouchard, M. (2010). Cleaning up your act: Forensic awareness as a detection avoidance strategy. *Journal of Criminal Justice, 38*, 1160–1166. doi: 10.1016/j.jcrimjus.2010.09.004

Beauregard, E., & Martineau, M. (2012). A descriptive study of sexual homicide in Canada: Implications for police investigation. *International Journal of Offender Therapy and Comparative Criminology, 57*(12), 1454–1476. doi: 10.1177/0306624X12456682

Beauregard, E., & Martineau, M. (2014). No body, no crime? The role of forensic awareness in avoiding police detection in cases of sexual homicide. *Journal of Criminal Justice, 42*, 213–220. doi: 10.1016/j.jcrimjus.2013.06.007

Bernard, T., & Snipes, J. (1996). Theoretical integration in criminology. *Crime and Justice: A Review of Research, 20*, 301–348.

Brown, K., & Keppel, R. (2012). Child abduction murder: The impact of forensic evidence on solvability. *Journal of Forensic Sciences, 57*(2), 353–353. doi:10.1111/j.1556–4029.2011.01970.x

Chase, K., O'Leary, K., & Heyman, R. (2001). Categorizing partner-violent men within the reactive-proactive typology model. *Journal of Consulting and Clinical Psychology, 69*, 567–572.

Cleckley, H. (1976). *The mask of sanity* (5th ed.). St. Louis, MO: Mosby.

Cole, S., & Diosa-Villa, R. (2007). *CSI* and its effects: Media, juries and the burden of proof. *New England Law Review, 41*, 435–469. Accessed October 31, 2016 from: http://ssrn.com/abstract=1023258

Cornish, D., & Clarke, R. (eds.) (1986). *The reasoning criminal: Rational choice perspectives on offending.* New York: Springer-Verlag.

Davies, A. (1992). Rapists' behaviour: A three aspect model as a basis for analysis and the identification of serial crime. *Forensic Science International, 55*, 173–194.

Durnal, E. (2010). Crime scene investigation (as seen on TV). *Forensic Science International, 199*, 1–5. doi: 10.1016/j.forsciint.2010.02.015

Eke, A. (2007). *Staging in cases of homicide: Offender victim and offence characteristics* (Unpublished Doctoral Thesis). York University.

Ferguson, C. (2015). Staged homicides: An examination of common features of faked burglaries, suicides, accidents and car accidents. *Journal of Police and Criminal Psychology*, 30(3), 139–157. doi: 10.1007/s11896-014-9154-1

Ferguson, C. (2018, September). *Forensically aware offenders and homicide investigations: Challenges, opportunities and impacts.* Paper presented at Australia and New Zealand Forensic Science Society Biennial Symposium, Perth, Australia.

Ferguson, C., & McKinley, A. (in press). The role of detection avoidance behaviour in solving Australian homicides: A proposed framework. *Salus Journal.*

Ferguson, C., & Pooley, K. (2019). Australian no-body homicides: Exploring common features of solved cases. *Journal of Forensic and Legal Medicine.* doi: 10.1016/j.jflm.2019.06.007

Ferguson C., & Sutherland, T. (2018). Murder by pushing: An exploratory analysis of homicidal falls from a height. *American Journal of Forensic Medicine and Pathology.* doi: 10.1097/PAF.0000000000000386

Geberth, V. (2006). *Practical homicide investigation: Tactics, procedures and forensic techniques* (4th ed.). Boca Raton, FL: CRC Press.

Hare, R. D. (1991). *The Hare psychopathy checklist-revised.* Toronto, ON: Multi-Health Systems, Inc.

Hare, R. D. (2003). *The Hare psychopathy checklist-revised* (2nd ed.). Toronto, ON: Multi Health Systems.

Hilton, N. Z., Harris, G. T., & Rice, M. E. (2010). *Risk assessment for domestically violent men: Tools for criminal justice, offender intervention, and victim services.* Washington, DC: American Psychological Association.

Ishikawa, S., Raine, A., Lencz, T., Bihrle, S., & LaCasse, L. (2001). Autonomic stress reactivity and executive functions in successful and unsuccessful criminal psychopaths from the community. *Journal of Abnormal Psychology, 110*, 423–432.

Jeffery, C., & Zahm, D. (1993). Crime prevention through environmental designs, opportunity theory, and rational choice models. In R. Clarke & M. Felson (Eds.), *Advances in criminological theory* (Vol. 5, pp. 323–350). New Brunswick, NJ: Transaction Press.

Monckton Smith, J. (2019). Intimate partner femicide: Using Foucauldian analysis to track an eight stage relationship progression to homicide. *Violence against Women*. doi: 10.1177%2F1077801219863876

Paternoster, R., & Simpson, S. (1996). Sanction threats and appeals to morality: Testing a rational choice model of corporate crime. *Law & Society Review, 30*, 378–399.

Pettler, L. (2011). *Crime scene behaviors of crime scene stagers* (Unpublished Doctoral Thesis). Capella University.

Piquero, A., & Tibbetts, S. (1996). Specifying the direct and indirect effects of low self-control and situational factors in offenders' decision making: Toward a more complete model of rational offending. *Justice Quarterly*, *13*, 481–510.

Porter, S., Doucette, N., Woodworth, M., Earle, J., & MacNeil, B. (2008). Halfe the world knows not how the other half lies: Investigation of verbal and non-verbal signs of deception exhibited by criminal offenders and non-offenders. *Legal and Criminological Psychology*, *13*, 27–38. doi: 10.1348/135532507X186653

Porter, S., & Woodworth, M. (2006). Psychopathy and aggression. In C. Patrick (Ed.), *Handbook of psychopathy* (pp. 481–494). New York: Guilford

Porter, S., & Woodworth, M. (2007). "I'm sorry I did it … but he started it": A comparison of the official and self-reported homicide descriptions of psychopaths and non-psychopaths. *Law & Human Behavior, 31*, 91–107. doi: 10.1007/s10979-006-9033-0

Porter, S., Woodworth, M., Earle, J., Drugge, J., & Boer, D. (2003). Characteristics of sexual homicides committed by psychopathic and non-psychopathic offenders. *Law and Human Behavior*, *27*(5), 459–470.

Reckless, W. (1961). A new theory of delinquency and crime. *Federal Probation, 25*, 42–46.

Salfati, G., & Haratsis, E. (2001). Greek homicide: A behavioral examination of offender crime scene actions. *Homicide Studies, 5*(4), 355–362. doi: 10.1177/1088767901005004006

Schlesinger, L., Gardenier, A., Jarvis, J., & Sheehan-Cook, J. (2012). Crime scene staging in homicide. *Journal of Police and Criminal Psychology, 29*, 44–51. doi: 10.1007/s11896-012-9114-6

Seto, M. C., & Barbaree, H. E. (1999). Psychopathy, treatment behavior, and sex offender recidivism. *Journal of Interpersonal Violence, 14,* 1235–1248.

Stevens, D. (2008). Forensic science, wrongful convictions and American prosecutor discretion. *The Howard Journal*, *47*(1), 31–51. doi: 10.1111/j.1468–2311.2008.00495.x

Tibbetts, S., & Gibson, C. (2002). Individual propensities and rational decision making: Recent findings and promising approaches. In Alex R. Piquero, and Stephen G. Tibbetts (Eds.), *Rational choice and criminal behavior: Recent research and future challenges*. New York: Routledge.

Woodworth, M., & Porter, S. (2002). In cold blood: Characteristics of criminal homicides as a function of psychopathy. *Journal of Abnormal Psychology, 111,* 436–445.

6 Toward a theory of detection avoidance as a form of coercive control

In the previous chapters, strong links between DA and IPH are demonstrated. In this chapter, links between coercive controlling behavior, IPF specifically and DA are made. It is argued that coercive control in relationships continues after an IPF in the form of DA, and that DA is used as a form of coercive control in planning and threatening the IPF. By exploring how and why IPHs occur and using numerous case examples, this chapter proposes that offenders use DA for more than just avoiding detection, to continue to control their victim(s) in both life and death. The use of DA provides attractive opportunities for offenders to control the narrative surrounding the victim's death, to blame victims, to take revenge on victims' loved ones and to enhance their own masculine status. A modified power and control wheel is offered to explain this relationship and provide examples of common offender DA behaviors in IPF cases. Overall, this chapter explores how IPF and DA are inextricably linked, and sometimes incredibly attractive to coercively controlling offenders.

In the last two decades, experts in domestic and family violence have begun to recognize controlling behaviors in relationships as risk factors for IPF (Stark, 2009). Even without physical violence, levels of controlling behaviors that are also coercive predict a woman's risk of being murdered much more than the severity or amount of physical assaults, because controlling behaviors undermine her capacity to resist or escape the abuse (Stark & Hester, 2019). According to Stark (2007, pp. 228–229), coercion is "the use of force or threats to compel or dispel a particular response" and control is "structural forms of deprivation, exploitation, and command that compel obedience indirectly". Together, the result is a "condition of unfreedom" (p. 205) similar to entrapment. Therefore, coercive control in relationships is defined as "a strategic course of self-interested behavior designed to secure and expand gender-based privilege by establishing a regime of domination in personal life" (Stark, 2012, p. 21). In Stark's work (2012, p. 21), this definition involves three elements: "the oppression is ongoing rather than episodic (a 'course of conduct') and resulting harms cumulative, that it is multifaceted, and that it involves rational, instrumental behavior". Examples of coercively controlling behaviors include limiting access to money, food, transportation, communication and micro-regulation of everyday behaviors such as how a person dresses, cares for their children or performs sexually (Stark, 2007). Importantly, Stark notes that perpetrators determine which tactics they use to control, isolate, intimidate and hurt victims through trial and error based on a cost–benefit analysis (Stark, 2012). Of course, this is not dissimilar to what has been said about DA behaviors as instrumental and based on a cost–benefit analysis by offenders, as proposed in Chapter 5.

The research described in Chapter 5 also shows that DA is more likely to occur in IPF cases where there is evidence of controlling behavior and where separation is threatened or the victim is trying to leave the offender (Eke, 2007). Other research explored in previous chapters shows clear links between DA and IPF or domestic and family violence homicides more broadly. Given these findings, it seems there is something about intimate relationships that encourages the use of DA aside from just a motivation to avoid detection. In the following discussion, DA in IPF is framed as a possible extension of coercively controlling behaviors in the relationship, where offenders manipulate evidence, investigators and witnesses in order to increase status, control the story surrounding the victims' death as well as their lives and punish victims and their families after the homicide. First, unpacking the basics of coercive control and its relationship to IPF provides clues as to how such behaviors initially manifest, and with whom.

Links between coercive control and violence

As mentioned, coercive control is a course of conduct where violence, controlling behavior, intimidation and isolation are tactics used by abusers to entrap their victims. In coercively controlling relationships, violence is used to prevent challenges to the abuser's control from surfacing rather than to resolve conflicts (Stark, 2012, p. 23). In this way, violence is used instrumentally to meet a desired end. In these relationships, isolation may also be used in a goal-oriented fashion, to alienate victims from their families, to keep women from accessing help and to prevent them from calling police to report abuse. The instrumentality of coercive control is common to motives behind IPF as well as the use of DA.

How an abuser specifically enacts violence, control, intimidation and isolation is specific to the abuser and the relationship, often based on his intimate knowledge of and ability to access personal information about his partner as a result of their relationship. This means that a myriad of specific strategies may be used to coercively control someone, making identifying, measuring and responding to these behaviors much more difficult for police and courts (Stark & Hester, 2019). Along with being dynamic, coercive control is also persistent. Ornstein and Rickne's (2013) research shows that violence as a form of coercive control is much more likely to persist after separation than violence without coercive control. Anderson (2005) adds that control itself may also continue even long after violence has stopped. Indeed, a relationship need not be physically or sexually violent to be coercively controlling. Lischick's (1999, 2009) findings demonstrate that a significant proportion of coercive controlling relationships do not ever involve violence. In such cases, other tactics, for example, threats of violence, may be enough to control the victim, and violence may not be necessary to reach the desired end (Dutton & Goodman, 2005). According to Dutton and Goodman (2005, p. 750), "Coercive control doesn't require a threatened consequence to be actually delivered—only creation of the belief that it could be". In fact, threats for noncompliance and other nonviolent behavior can be more powerful than physical violence because male control over female partners is socially acceptable in many contexts where physical violence is not, and control therefore may not be seen as problematic or signaling risk (Johnson, Eriksson, Mazerolle, & Wortley, 2019).

Violence may only be used only when control is perceived to be ebbing (Dobash & Dobash, 2015). Indeed, in some relationships ending in homicide, violence has never been used prior to the murder (Johnson, Eriksson, Mazerolle, & Wortley, 2019). In those cases that are violent, coercively controlling violence can be more severe and more frequent than other forms of violence (Johnson, 2008). Several studies have also shown that coercively controlling behaviors can precede, cause or increase the likelihood of violence in relationships (Graham-Kevan & Archer, 2008; Hardesty et al., 2015); however, with or without violence, the dynamics and consequences of coercive control are similar (Crossman, Hardesty, & Raffaelli, 2016).

Coercive control, status and IPF

The research on IPF demonstrates an undeniable link between coercive control and homicide, where coercive control is nine times more effective in predicting homicide than threats and violence (Stark, 2009). Coercive control appears to be a predictive factor for IPF, perhaps due to its course of conduct rather than the specific techniques used. Research on stalking and IPF has shown coercive control is often fixated and obsessive in nature, especially when it results in a homicide (Monckton Smith, Szymanska, & Haile, 2017). In these cases, otherwise low-level controlling behaviors become a higher risk for homicide when they are persistent and continuous (Monckton Smith et al., 2017; Stark, 2009). Research on IPF and stalking also indicates that controlling and intimidating behaviors preceding a homicide may be versatile, with offenders changing control and intimidation behaviors as the circumstances and victim resistance dictates (Monckton Smith et al., 2017). Fixation on the goal of controlling, intimidating or punishing the victim seems to be key, with offenders being flexible and resourceful in the tactics used to meet that end. Such a fixation along with an offender's willingness to change tactics are important findings, given the argument that an offender may continue to try to exert control over the victim even after he has murdered her. That is, since offenders are fixated on exacting revenge or attempting to regain control over the victim prior to the homicide, DA behaviors before and after it may be motivated by this fixation as well, at least in part. More is said of this below. First, why and when coercively controlling relationships become lethal, as relevant to the discussion of DA are briefly outlined.

When does IPF occur?

IPF is associated with separation or threats to leave the relationship in the majority of cases (Dobash & Dobash, 2015; Monckton Smith, 2019). Dobash and Dobash (2015, p. 39) explain that a key feature of IPF is the man deciding to "change the project" from attempting to regain control of the victim in the relationship to "destroying her for leaving it". Of particular note is the element of decision involved, where the project is changed after some deliberation rather than uncontrollable emotions or "snapping" on the part of the offender. High levels of planning by offenders, often found in IPF cases, are strong evidence of this decision-making (Monckton Smith, 2019). Monckton Smith's (2019) work highlights the apparent decision-making process, noting that no matter how rapidly the decision might be made, it is made nonetheless. Like coercive controlling behaviors more generally, this "last chance thinking" points to instrumentality in the homicide rather than escalating violence that went too far in a highly emotional situation. In this way, IPF occurs when offenders come to believe that they have no way to mitigate their feelings of outrage and injustice, and since control cannot be regained, there is to their minds nothing left for them besides homicide. Like the fixation seen in attempting to regain control of the victim in the relationship, recent findings show that "last chance thinking" about exacting revenge or punishing the victim is similarly rigid and fixated (Monckton Smith, 2019). In these cases, offenders may go to great lengths to perpetrate the murder, using various tactics to manipulate time alone with the victim, gaining access to weapons and/or being ready to act should the opportunity present itself (Monckton Smith, 2019).

Why does IPF occur?

Why offenders decide to change the project and kill their partner has been theorized in the literature for a number of years. Early theories viewed separation as an extreme public challenge to the male partner (Ellis & DeKeseredy, 1997; Wilson & Daly, 1992). These theories positioned male partners as having proprietary views of women, believing that they have every right to control women, and thus attempt to reinstate control when control is threatened through separation (Ellis & DeKeseredy, 1997; Wilson & Daly, 1992). More recent literature builds on this, associating "last chance thinking" with "feelings of injustice, entitlement to act, and a belief that there is social or cultural solidarity with the offender's position" (Monckton Smith,

2019, p. 20). In more contemporary theories, IPF is borne out of feelings that the offender is the real victim, and that loss of control of a female partner results in a loss of status.

Much of this theorizing comes from explanations of IPV more broadly as resulting from a threat to masculine status, or simply how some men "do gender" (Peralta & Tuttle, 2013). For example, Peralta and Tuttle (2013) describe IPV as a way to express masculinity, compared with other (perhaps less accessible) expressions, such as gainful employment or power in the workplace. Anderson and Umberson's (2001) interviews with 33 men found IPV was used to reinstate or maintain the gender order (i.e., male domination/female subordination), and Melzer's (2002) work describes IPV as a way to compensate for perceived shortcomings in masculine status. Anderson (2005) explains that IPV becomes more likely if men perceive their masculinity as threatened, especially when other mechanisms for gender expression are not available. In Wood's (2004, p. 569) interviews with 22 men, it was noted that participants' patriarchal views of manhood were associated with feelings of entitlement to control relationships and women, and to use IPV to "enforce their male entitlements". Finally, in a US study of intimate partner abusers, men expressed that controlling their partners was their right and that punishments for exercising this right were unjust, making men the true victims (Guzik, 2008).

If violence and control is seen as a way to express masculinity, then internalized implications of what loss of control means to the male identity (such as loss of property ownership, money, father/husband status, reputation) may result in a perceived loss of status when control is ebbing (Peralta & Tuttle, 2013). If control is threatened through separation or other triggers, perpetrators may attempt to prevent status being lost, regain it or exact revenge to even the playing field.

Evidence supporting the role of revenge, loss of control and status in IPF cases abounds. For example, Monckton Smith's (2019, p. 18) work in the UK specifically associates losing the ability to control partners through separation with a perceived loss of status. After threatened or real separation, offenders in this sample attempted to regain control through escalating violence. When it became apparent that control would not be regained, offenders decided to kill the victim as punishment or for revenge (Monckton Smith, 2019). Johnson et al. (2019, p. 7) studied the role of coercive control in femicides and found that these murders were commonly triggered by a loss of control due to separation or perceived infidelity. These homicides often took place in a context of male possessiveness, extreme jealousy, attempts to isolate women and threats of suicide or homicide. Juodis, Starzomski, Porter and Woodworth's (2014) comparison of intimate and non-intimate femicides in Canada similarly showed that men who killed their partners were more often motivated by a desire to inflict pain and suffering out of revenge. These homicides often took place over a backdrop of women instigating separation and beginning a new relationship, disputes over divorce and child custody and more broadly, male proprietariness and jealousy.

To summarize, IPF and offenders changing the project from trying to regain control to exacting revenge appear to be linked to masculine status, feelings of justification for the lethal behavior and injustice for their own treatment. Offenders may be fixated on punishing victims or regaining lost status, so they decide to kill and may plan ahead or manipulate opportunities to perpetrate the homicide. Given the instrumentality of coercively controlling behaviors involved in IPF as well as instrumental DA explored in previous chapters, it is possible that offenders use DA during an IPF for more than just avoiding detection. The following section proposes that offenders use DA as a vehicle for control during an IPF: to influence perceptions of victims, their proxies and the things that were important to them; to take revenge on their memory and their helpers; and to regain, retain or enhance their masculine status.

DA as form of coercive control

Studies specific to DA have shown clear links between CSS and controlling behaviors (Eke, 2007). In Eke's study of IPF and psychopathy in Canada discussed in the last chapter, offenders using CSS used more coercively controlling behaviors in the relationship prior to the homicide than those not using staging, including controlling or attempting to control things such as finances, sex, the victim's time with friends or family and what clothing they wear. In Eke's (2007) sample, 32% of staging offenders had IPV-related charges before the homicide, which is lower than the rates found among more general IPF samples in Ontario, Canada, where the sample was gathered. Since offenders eventually used violence to kill the victim, this finding perhaps speaks to the type of abusive relationships preceding homicides and which involve DA/CSS, in which victims do not report physical violence or psychological violence and control. Not unlike more general findings in IPF cases, many victims in Eke's (2007) staged and not staged cases were separated or planning to separate from the offender when they were murdered. Furthermore, staged cases were significantly more likely to involve the victim planning to separate from the offender rather than already being separated at the time of the offense. Stagers were also significantly more likely to be married to victims than their non-staging counterparts. Combined with findings related to personality and PCL-R scores as well as what is known about IPF more broadly, this result may speak to the risk associated with married victims threatening or planning to leave abusive partners with these personality traits. Such findings also demonstrate the associated motives, deliberation, manipulation of evidence and attempted control over the investigation used by DA offenders in IPF cases.

In the literature on IPV and homicide more broadly, coercive controlling violence is more likely to persist *after separation* than other types of violence and coercive controlling behaviors may continue long after violence has ceased (Anderson, 2003; Ornstein & Rickne, 2013). It is proposed here that coercively controlling behavior may even continue after a woman has been murdered by her partner, and this control is facilitated through the use of DA by the offender. In this way, DA behaviors are used as a vehicle for control. This can involve using DA to manipulate investigators, family, friends and the legal system (family, civil, criminal) for one's own benefit. Along with simply avoiding detection, DA behaviors are used by perpetrators to control the narrative surrounding the relationship and the victim's life and death; to reinstate control over things shared between victims and offenders (such as children, property); to punish the victim's proxies for her/their noncompliance; and/or to save face or reinstate lost masculine status. Evidence of DA being used as a vehicle of control comes from several key findings, including different qualities and quantities of DA expended by IPF offenders in comparison to other types of homicide offenders; offenders using DA to continue to manipulate the legal system after the murder; offenders' eagerness to engage with authorities to establish their innocence and her responsibility for her death; and offenders using the innocent façade to control access to the victim's body and funeral arrangements. The evidence of each of these behaviors is discussed below, with examples from the DA literature. Following this, a modified version of The Duluth Model's power and control wheel is presented to summarize some of the key DA behaviors used as a vehicle for coercive control during an IPF (www.theduluthmodel.org).

DA is different in IPF

While most murderers would presumably prefer to avoid detection, IPF offenders use more and different DA behaviors than other offenders perpetrating domestic and family violence homicides or stranger homicides (Ferguson, 2015, 2016; Ferguson et al., 2015; Ferguson & Petherick, 2016; Ferguson & Sutherland, 2018). This finding suggests that IPF offenders approach DA in a way that is different to other homicide offenders. Variations in DA behaviors are especially pronounced when it comes to the quantity of tactics used and whether those, and the homicide, are planned in advance.

For example, in their analysis of stranger sexual homicide offenders, Beauregard and Martineau (2014) found that when used, most offenders employed only one strategy to avoid detection, such as wearing a condom, disposing of the victim's body and so on. The same cannot be said of offenders perpetrating IPF. The literature on DA indicates that domestic and family homicides (including IPF) have the greatest number of moderate and elaborate staging levels out of all types of homicides (Schlesinger et al., 2012). Research specific to IPFs involving DA shows that these homicides most often involve five DA behaviors, five times more than stranger sexual homicides (Beauregard & Martineau, 2014; Ferguson, 2018). Such findings point to the relationship between victims and offenders having important links to which and how many DA behaviors are used.

As discussed in previous chapters, Beauregard and Martineau (2014) explain that stranger sex offenders use few DA behaviors because of the cognitive load these offenders bear while committing a homicide. If this is the case, cognitive load may be lower for IPF offenders because of access to crime scenes, but also how they feel about killing the victim. That is, decisions made by offenders regarding their use of DA may be impacted by factors discussed above, including the offender's rigid fixation on punishing the victim, their high need for control, feeling indignant that they are the true victim of their partner's noncompliance, a perceived solidarity with their position and/or a view that homicide is the only choice they have left (Monckton Smith, 2019). Indeed, the decision to kill associated with IPF in the literature suggests that cognitive load may not be so high as to limit offenders using DA in these cases. Since deliberate decision-making is known to precede IPF cases, cognitive load may also be reduced by offenders' ability to plan the homicide and the DA ahead of time, based on their intimate knowledge of the victim (Dobash & Dobash, 2015). The research available on DA supports strong links between planning the IPF itself and the DA, suggesting that greater levels of DA in these cases may be due to offenders planning both in advance, when cognitive load is lower.

In Ferguson's (2015) examination of 115 staged homicides (63 staged IPH), there was evidence that 36% of the murders were planned in advance (note that levels of planning were unknown in the majority of cases). Planning was determined by offenders bringing weapons to the scene or the presence of DA before the homicide, such as by securing an alibi. In other samples involving IPH or IPF specifically, even higher proportions of homicides involving DA were planned. For example, in a sample of homicides concealed as accidental falls from a height, 83% of the IPH cases studied were planned in advance, such as by scouting potential fall sites and creating detailed ruses to lure the victim there (Ferguson & Sutherland, 2018). In homicides perpetrated by offenders with police training, 54% were known to have been planned, as evidenced by offenders buying supplies, and telling friends or even victims of their plans (Ferguson, 2018). Excerpts from court documents pertaining to offenders with police training illustrate strong links between deliberate decision-making in IPF cases and DA behaviors, where the murder and how to get away with it appear to be planned in tandem. For example, in an IPF involving a woman who was attempting to separate from her husband, court transcripts revealed: "A close friend of [offender], testified that approximately one month prior to the disappearance of [victim], [offender] told him he was 'going to kill that bitch and throw her in the woods'". This was not an idle threat on the part of the offender, as the victim's body was not discovered until after he was convicted of her murder in the very woods he had indicated to the witness. Cases such as this illustrate that while the exact timing of the homicide may not be anticipated by offenders, the homicidal plan and the DA go together and are clearly set out in advance. In this case, after the offender was unable to regain control of the victim, he acted out his threatened plan to punish her and (attempt to) remain undetected (Ferguson, 2018).

In other cases, the offender's threats reveal both the way that the threat itself is used to control the victim as well as the planning of the murder and how the offender will get away with it. In one case in Ferguson's (2018) police-trained sample of offenders:

> [A witness] testified that [offender] had offered [witness] $25,000 … to find someone to kill [victim] … About six weeks before [victim's] death, [victim] came to [her sister's] house in the afternoon unexpectedly and was afraid and upset. [Sister] asked [victim] what was wrong. [Victim] stated that [offender] had told her that he was going to kill her, that she was not going to make it to the divorce settlement, and that she was not going to get his pension or the children. [Offender] had stated further that he was going to kill [victim] and make it look like an accident.

The perpetrator in this case subsequently did exactly that, making the victim's death appear as though she drowned in her own bathtub (Ferguson, 2018). This murder was erroneously ruled an accidental death and misclassified for a period of years, until the offender's second wife went missing after she voiced her suspicions about the death of the first victim (Ferguson, 2018). The offender was subsequently convicted of the murder of his first wife, while his second wife remains a long-term missing person. This case shows the strong link between DA and the homicide in this offender's planning, where the two were inextricably linked and his intentions for both the homicide and DA were clearly articulated in advance.

In a particularly harrowing example of a planned DA homicide, the offender intended to murder his wife before she had the chance to separate from him and prearranged to dispose of her body with a woodchipper. The court remarked:

> As part of the defendant's plan, prior to the events of [the night the victim was murdered] he had arranged for the rental of a woodchipper, the purchase of a truck with which to haul the woodchipper, and the purchase of a large freezer … Upon a more detailed search of areas containing the woodchip debris, the police found pieces of bone and tissue, a human fingernail and crowns to the victim's teeth
>
> (Ferguson, 2018).

The victim in this case was aware that the perpetrator was actively planning her murder. At the trial:

> the state presented the testimony of five witnesses who offered statements made by the victim during the [season she was killed]. [The victim's attorney] handling the divorce proceeding, testified that the victim

> had told her that "if something should happen to her I should not assume that it was an accident." [A coworker and friend] testified that the victim had told her that "her husband would find her wherever she went… [and that] he would have an alibi and a well thought out plan"; [this witness'] husband testified to the same effect. [Another co-worker] testified that the victim had told her that "if anything ever happens to me, please don't accept it as an accident no matter what he says
>
> (Ferguson, 2018)

By showing that the homicide and DA are planned in tandem and in advance, these examples illustrate that increased levels of DA in IPF cases are likely to be related to the deliberate decision to kill preceding these homicides (Monckton Smith, 2019). When such decision-making occurs, feelings associated with offenders' "changing the project" may impact on cognitive load, perhaps decreasing it by enhancing the offenders' perceptions of being justified or having no other choice. Likewise, an offender's ability to use his intimate knowledge of the victim to plan the DA ahead of time may also reduce cognitive load during the commission of the murder, increasing his ability to carry out more DA behaviors or providing opportunities for some behaviors to be done ahead of time.

Using DA to manipulate the legal system

It is clear that offenders choose to use DA as part of their decision to kill their partner and that they do so in different ways than non-IPF offenders. As described above, it is proposed that this difference comes from a desire to not only avoid detection for the murder, but also to continue to control the victim and relationship and to regain masculine status after the death. Support for this proposition is found in evidence that offenders' attempts to manipulate the legal system for their own benefit continue after an IPF, using the façade they have attempted to portray through DA behaviors.

It is well documented that many women experiencing IPV feel that their partners manipulate the legal system to hide or minimize abuse, intimidate and frighten them or to make them look untrustworthy (DeKeseredy and Schwartz, 2009; Douglas & Stark, 2010; Monckton Smith et al., 2017). For example, Douglas and Stark (2010) interviewed women and noted that:

> many women expressed deep frustration at their partner's ability to manipulate them and 'work the system'. They spoke of deliberate tactics to conceal or disguise (physical) evidence of abuse, to 'charm' outsiders and to misrepresent the reality of their experience … Women believed that police and magistrates were often conned and manipulated by the perpetrator's behavior
>
> (Douglas & Stark, 2010, p. 26)

Clearly, some victims of IPV believe these manipulative tactics are successful for abusers, which enhances the likelihood of offenders continuing to use them in the future. Evidence shows that such behaviors may be used after separation and/or prior to an IPF as well. For example, Monckton Smith and colleagues (2017, p. 5) comment on the regular use of vexatious litigation and baseless reports by perpetrators preceding IPFs in their sample. Such manipulation of police and the family court is instrumental and multifaceted for offenders as it forces contact with victims, instills fear and control and can make the victim appear unstable or untrustworthy (Monckton Smith et al., 2017). At the time they are perpetrated, these activities are rarely recognized as manipulating the system to control or stalk the victim (Monckton Smith et al., 2017).

Similarly, there are numerous versatile examples of such controlling and manipulative behaviors after an IPF when the murder is concealed through DA, often working to help offenders avoid detection or punishment. As examples, offenders may request civil orders to protect them from their victim's family, thus reinforcing their own perceived victimhood and bolstering negative claims about the deceased victim and her loved ones. They may work quickly to secure life insurance proceeds, to dispose of mutual assets or to hide funds before they are suspected, arrested and charged with the homicide. After arrest, perpetrators may enlist family members to attempt to secure custody of or access to children shared with the victim; they may use the system to tie up funds that would otherwise go to the victim's children or surviving family; or they may attempt to delay or derail criminal proceedings with numerous appeals, motions, outbursts or claims of mental illness. In other cases, offenders may use suicide attempts or threats to manipulate the system or create delays, to get special treatment in jail or as an attempt to appear remorseful and reduce sentences (Eke, 2007).

All these behaviors work to control the situation and intimidate those involved, sometimes effectively preventing others from acting against the offender. Even post-conviction, offenders may continue manipulating the system to control or harm victims' families through continued denials or refusal to reveal the location of the victim's body. For example, Ferguson and Pooley's (2019) study of no body homicides, discussed in Chapter 2, found several cases where offenders' use of DA allowed them to minimize their culpability after they were arrested and charged. These offenders originally denied any knowledge of the victim's disappearance, but eventually alleged that they killed the victim accidentally before disposing of the body, thus reducing their charge from murder to manslaughter. One such offender even "confessed" to where he disposed of his victim in order to feign cooperation with police and the courts. His claims were shown to be untrue and her body has not been recovered; however, the perpetrator was still only convicted of manslaughter based on his supposed admissions and cooperation. This lesser charge was despite the offender threatening to cut off the victim's head in the hours before she disappeared (Ferguson & Pooley, 2019). Even when unsuccessful in avoiding detection completely, such examples illustrate the power DA allows offenders to wield over the ensuing investigation and their own prosecution, creating delays, reducing charges, controlling those involved or influencing family and civil court decisions. This desire to control the situation and actors involved appears very similar to the coercive control exerted over victims prior to their homicide, suggesting that offenders are motivated to continue attempts at control even after murdering the victim.

The case of Robert Peernock provides a startling example of the type of control DA behaviors allow offenders to exercise using the criminal, civil and family court systems. In July 1987, days before his estranged wife was set to refile for divorce, Peernock attacked his wife and teenaged daughter, doused them with gasoline and staged a car accident with the intention of concealing their murders (Quinn, 1991). Fortunately, the elaborate staging was unsuccessful. Natasha Peernock, aged 18, survived and reported the death of her mother as murder (Moran, 1991). Under suspicion by police, Peernock began manipulating the system in an attempt to derail the criminal investigation, bolster his ability to defend himself and ensure that anyone surviving his late wife would not benefit financially – not even their shared children. Such manipulations were all rationalized by the offender as necessary to prove that his wife had died in a car accident and that his surviving daughter was not credible. According to a book written about the case, Peernock removed cash from accounts and transferred it into accounts under others' names (Flacco, 1995). He continued stalking his surviving daughter while evading police in an effort to intimidate her and prevent her cooperating with the investigation. After his arrest, he delayed his trial by firing four consecutive attorneys, appealing to higher courts to allow him to represent himself, suing judges and his own attorney and so on. These efforts prevented the criminal trial from commencing for three years. While awaiting trial, he also appealed numerous decisions in the family court regarding custody and access to his younger daughter with the victim. He similarly appealed decisions regarding their shared property and her numerous life insurance policies, often representing himself from jail and under the guise of his being falsely charged after an accidental death. Doing so allowed him access to otherwise protected information, which he used to intimidate friends and family of the victims. His self-representation also provided him an opportunity to cross-examine his surviving daughter for four days during a custody decision appeal, mostly regarding her credibility about his efforts at DA. This cross-examination was often sarcastic, intimidating and hostile, bringing a number of reprimands from the presiding judge (Flacco, 1995). In his criminal trial, Peernock made continuous outbursts in an attempt to disrupt the trial, garnering repeated warnings (Flacco, 1995).

The impact of these manipulative efforts on detecting, arresting and prosecuting Peernock for his crimes was far-reaching. Peernock successfully delayed his arrest, prosecution and conviction (Quinn, 1991). He manipulated ways to access his surviving victim and confront her publicly (Flacco, 1995). This was designed to benefit his various court cases, minimize his abuse in the marriage, dismiss and belittle her experiences, and intimidate her and others into accepting the accident scenario and no longer cooperating with police. His efforts to inundate his daughter's attorneys with baseless motions and correspondence effectively prevented her accessing any of her mother's estate for a period of years, also preventing her from using any of these funds for her mother's funeral or her own recovery and further instilling fear (Flacco, 1995). Thus, these tactics also reserved these funds for the perpetrator's use should the DA be successful and he be acquitted. Fortunately, Peernock's DA efforts were ultimately unsuccessful, and he was eventually convicted for the IPF of his estranged wife and for attempted murder of his daughter, along with arson, kidnapping and solicitation of two additional murders (Moran, 1991).

Although this example is extreme, it provides a useful illustration of how an offender's use of DA can facilitate coercive controlling behaviors continuing after an IPF.

Offenders' engagement with authorities

More support for DA being used to control the situation after an IPF comes from the literature on IPF offenders' eagerness to engage with authorities following attempts to conceal a homicide.

Bancroft (2002, p. 137) notes that "abusive men are drawn to power and control, and part of how they get it is by looking good in public". Saving face in public, or indeed regaining masculine status, appears to be a key motivator in IPF cases involving DA. In these cases, the façade set up by the offender may be the first step in regaining status after a real or threatened separation. The second step involves engaging with police to establish the narrative of the façade as the reality of the death – usually involving portraying the victim negatively and the offender positively. Establishing this narrative requires offenders to engage and cooperate with police, and often includes attempts to manipulate investigators so that perpetrators appear as sympathetic, believable, nice guys. Such behaviors are well practiced for many intimate partner abusers, with much evidence indicating that IPV offenders manipulate police responding to domestic violence reports. For example, in Douglas and Stark's (2010, p. 49) work discussed earlier, "interviewees commented on the apparently friendly relationship between police and perpetrators. According to interviewees on many occasions, police officers seemed to have great empathy toward perpetrators". Other research has similarly noted the social connections that exist between police and perpetrators (Websdale & Johnson, 1997, p. 312). In one study, survivors called for the "breaking up of the good ol' boy network that protected the offender" (DeKeseredy & Schwartz, 2009, p. 107). Illustrating the power of these manipulative behaviors, one woman interviewed by Douglas and Stark (2010, p. 49) explained that her abuser would immediately control how he was perceived by police by using politeness and niceties. The woman explained:

> [police]turn up and he's like uh and runs outside and goes, oh yeah, officer, don't worry about it. There's nothing going on and all this sort of stuff. They go oh what a nice guy. You know how guys are like that? They're all like oh what a great guy. He seems really nice
>
> (Douglas & Stark, 2010, p. 49)

When it comes to IPF and DA, offenders appear to use similar tactics to develop rapport with police and increase the believability of their version of events surrounding their partner's death. In Eke's (2007) work, almost all offenders immediately made themselves available for interview by police. Given the seriousness of the offence and the corresponding pressure on offenders, their willingness to be interviewed immediately at the scene or after being given the death notification is noteworthy. Such behavior highlights an important difference between IPF offenders using DA and other murderers, who may go to great lengths to avoid ever interacting with authorities (Eke, 2007). It is significant to note that for the few offenders in Eke's (2007) research who were not immediately available for interview, their unavailability made up part of the false narrative of the death – they were hiding from people who were trying to kill them but got their partner instead; they were on a business trip and she was home alone and vulnerable; they were injured in the accident that killed their partner; or they were out looking for her.

Motivation to engage with authorities immediately despite the risk involved appears to come from an offender's desire to control the narrative surrounding the victim's death. Offenders engage with police to establish an innocent scenario for the death from the outset, often involving maligning the victim and building themselves up. For example, offenders commonly report that victims died by suicide, accident or have simply disappeared. In the case of suicide, this often involves the victim being characterized by the offender as depressed, mentally ill, unstable and/or abandoning her children. In accidental scenarios, offenders commonly describe victims as clumsy, accident-prone, drunk, risk-taking, attention-seeking or not listening to advice. Victims who have disappeared are commonly reported to have run off with another man, being sick of motherhood or simply on extended vacation while fathers are left to look after shared children. Along with these negative characterizations of victims of concealed IPF, offenders also commonly attempt to control how they are perceived by police and the public as well. Offenders frame themselves as good fathers, picking up the slack for absentee mothers, attempting to help the victim or heroic in the moments before and after her death. In so doing, an offender undermines the status of their victim and increases his own status. Controlling the narrative of the death has the added benefit of allowing offenders an opportunity to save face, reframing the relationship, minimizing victims' attempts to separate or chocking the whole situation up to issues with the victim rather than with his controlling abuse.

Ferguson's (2018) police-trained IPF offenders' study reports on one perpetrator who killed the mother of his small children after she separated from him. Despite telling friends that she knew he was planning her murder, police did not investigate her disappearance as a homicide, and he was not convicted for nearly two decades. The way this offender explained the victim's disappearance and his own behavior at the time alludes to his desire to save face. Court documents reveal:

> [Offender] told investigators and others that [victim] had decided to take a trip to reconsider whether to stay in the marriage. [Offender] specified that he had met with [victim] on April 23 and 24 to give her money for the trip... And if her motive was greed and a carefree life, as [offender] suggested, she would not have left money behind at the condo and in her bank accounts, and she would not have accepted $25,000 from [offender] when she was entitled to $250,000 in community property.
>
> (Ferguson, 2018)

The judge also remarked that "his extremely negative comments about her after she disappeared showed that he was deeply angry with her for leaving him and for having sex with someone else". In this case, the offender capitalized on a number of opportunities to malign the victim while characterizing himself as a loving single dad who had tried to help the victim by giving her money for a vacation (Ferguson, 2018). These manipulations worked for a period of years. Her body has never been found.

In other cases, the offender provides a detailed story of how the death occurred in order to cast the victim in a negative light and himself as heroic. In one such case:

> the accused stated he was then in the kitchen and saw [victim] run to the balcony and step over the railing onto an outer ledge. He said, 'I ran toward the railing and, I can't remember, I was just trying to hold her from falling. I was just grabbing at her, I don't know, I might have had her handbag or jacket, then she was gone'
>
> (Ferguson & Sutherland, 2018, p. 5)

This offender indicated that the victim climbed over the balcony railing on the 15th floor of the high-rise apartment (with her handbag) as an attention-seeking behavior, and that her packed bags and stated intentions to leave him that morning were empty threats. In court, the judge remarked:

> The [defendant's] alternative suggestion that [the victim] took that step [over the balcony] in order to frighten him or as a cry for attention may

> be dismissed as fanciful. [The victim] may have been impulsive, maladaptive and oversensitive; she may have been in a state of acute fear and despair but I do not think she was deranged
>
> (Ferguson & Sutherland, 2018, p. 5)

In a strikingly similar IPF, the offender stated to police investigators:

> I was in the kitchen and I heard [victim]. I don't remember what I heard, I don't know if she called my name or not, I heard a noise, all I know is I ran when I heard it. I know it was something important enough to catch my attention and I ran like hell. I went out through the south exit. As I came around the corner, she was starting to fall backwards and I—she was already falling, I ran to the balcony and all of the way over to the railing and I reached over and I had her. I had my arms around her, I couldn't hang on. She was trying to reach me but she couldn't hang on. She was slipping, I was trying to hang on. I even had her arm at one point but I couldn't hang on. She just slipped away. She was gasping. She fell right out of my hands. I believe, I think, I am not sure, it was her right arm. I believe it was around her waist I grabbed first... She was already over the balcony, we were face to face, I remember looking at her face, I was leaning over the rail, I was too weak to hold onto her and she fell
>
> (Ferguson & Sutherland, 2018, p. 6)

Along with being demonstrably impossible, this narrative aimed to position the offender as deserving sympathy from police. The offender later indicated that he had instructed the victim not to stand on a stool on the balcony. She had done so anyway, and despite his supposed heroic efforts to save her, she had died in the "accidental" fall (Ferguson & Sutherland, 2018).

In another example from Ferguson's (2018) work, the offender attempted to explain his wife's gunshot wound as resulting from a suicide due to a completely fabricated illness related to the birth of their child. The offender stated to police that after giving birth to their infant son:

> It was requested that [victim] be bedridden for almost two months and that failure to follow these instructions exactly would result in continued free bleeding from her vaginal tear. As it occurred, [victim] heeded this advice and I was left to attend to [the infant's] every need...
>
> (Ferguson, 2018)

Even when explaining his wife's alleged suicide, this offender takes an opportunity to make himself look like a noble husband and father, perhaps using the intimate nature of such an injury to prevent investigators asking further questions. In the same case, the victim's doctor testified that she "never ordered [victim] to be on bed rest, and there were no indications that [victim] could not take care of her baby or that she was non-functioning. [Doctor] testified that [offender's] statements regarding [victim's] pregnancy were untrue" (Ferguson, 2018).

As these examples illustrate, regardless of the level of detail provided in offenders' accounts of the victim's death or disappearance, attempts to control the narrative surrounding her life and death are evident. Offenders use DA to create chances to malign the victim's character, blame her for the death and minimize her reports of abuse or attempts to leave the relationship. They also exploit opportunities to frame themselves positively as heroes, helpers, good husbands and loving dads. As seen in the two examples of homicides by throwing the victim from a height, these efforts go beyond simply providing an innocent scenario for the death to avoid detection. In these cases, the DA is also used to increase the offender's status and undermine the victim.

Offenders controlling death arrangements

Finally, DA as a vehicle of control after an IPF is perhaps most strongly evidenced by offenders' attempts to control what happens to their victim's body. While desiring to have a victim quickly cremated is useful for offenders attempting to avoid detection, it is also high risk, in that the order may signal to family, friends and authorities that an offender is attempting to escape scrutiny. This is especially true if the arrangements made by the offender are demonstrably against the victim's stated wishes. So, why do offenders risk signaling their DA to others by going against the deceased's stated wishes if attempting to appear innocent? It is theorized that doing so offers an attractive opportunity for offenders to control the victim's death, perhaps fulfilling a desire for revenge against the victim or their proxies. Offenders may use other coercively controlling behaviors as a way to justify their actions. For example, offenders may use a victim's isolation from family and friends to rationalize that these loved ones do not know what the victim would have wanted, or to explain that he was the only person who knew the "real" victim.

Many examples of offenders controlling arrangements after a victim's death exist in the DA literature. As one exemplar, an offender pushed his victim from a deck causing her a significant head injury. When she did not immediately die from this injury, he pushed her unconscious body into the water, where she drowned. The victim in this case was attempting to separate from the offender, and he had grave concerns about what divorce would mean for his ability to give marriage counseling advice as part of his business. This offender immediately sought to control police and family access to his wife's belongings and their children. As stated in the court documents:

> [the] defendant was preparing to leave and had already packed the family's belongings [and children] into the vehicle when victim's [sic] body

> had not even been removed... Defendant wished to have victim's [sic] body immediately cremated... Defendant's desire to have the body cremated could be viewed as an effort to destroy evidence of the crime of murder
>
> (Ferguson & Sutherland, 2018, p. 6)

Though appearing cooperative, this offender immediately began gatekeeping the access of family, friends and authorities in order to maintain control of the "accidental" narrative surrounding the death. Two cases of fatal falls from a height that were planned in detail by the corresponding offenders in order to avoid a costly divorce provide further examples. In the first case, family members were not allowed to see the victim's body or say goodbye to her, and the offender insisted on having the victim cremated against her and her family's clearly indicated wishes. Court documents indicate that the "[defendant] was eager to have [the victim] quickly cremated, despite family requests against it" (Ferguson & Sutherland, 2018, p. 6). The offender explained that cremation was decided based on his understanding of the victim's wishes that her family were not privy to. In the second case, the offender attempted to prevent his wife's death being reported in the media, despite her being fairly high-profile in their community and having many friends. The police investigation later revealed that this offender had a previous wife who also died in a suspicious accident. She too was immediately cremated, and her death was not ruled suspicious nor investigated as a homicide (Ferguson & Sutherland, 2018). This history of a dead spouse may provide a rationale for the offender avoiding making the victim's death public, despite she and her family's wishes.

While helping offenders avoid detection, controlling arrangements for the victim's funeral and interment also provide offenders with an opportunity to hurt or punish her friends and family. Offenders call upon coercively controlling behaviors in the relationship to rationalize these behaviors, such as victims' having little contact with their families prior to their deaths.

Based on the evidence outlined above, it is proposed that IPF offenders use DA in two ways. First, like many offenders, they are motivated to avoid detection and to not be held responsible for their crimes. However, unlike other types of murderers, IPF offenders use DA as a vehicle to persist with controlling the victim and her proxies in death, as in life. DA appears to be an integral part of the decision-making involved in many IPF cases, where it is used to manipulate and frustrate the legal system so that the offender is not held to account, to establish a self-serving narrative of the death portraying him positively and blaming her and to hurt or punish her family by controlling arrangements surrounding her death. These are only the most blatant examples of DA as a vehicle for control. To summarize these and other DA behaviors used to control victims in death, a modified version of The Duluth Model's power and control wheel is useful (www.theduluthmodel.org). This wheel presents common controlling DA

Figure 6.1 Power and control surrounding concealed IPF.

behaviors used by offenders to manipulate, control and intimidate investigators, witnesses, family, children and the system. This proposal is based on the author's research and consultancy on IPF cases using DA. Although many examples exist of other controlling DA behaviors, these are the most common seen in the literature and the author's case work (Figure 6.1).

Conclusion

When IPF is perpetrated, it commonly involves an offender deciding to "change the project", from trying to control a victim to punishing her or exacting revenge for noncompliance (Dobash & Dobash, 2015). Though such a decision may be made rapidly, it is made deliberately nonetheless (Monckton Smith, 2019). This decision appears to be linked to masculine status, feelings of justification for the lethal behavior and injustice for their own treatment (Monckton Smith, 2019). Offenders may be fixated on carrying out the homicide and may therefore plan to do so in advance. Offenders' planning how they will avoid detection appears to go hand in hand with planning the homicide, meaning that offenders may perpetrate DA after deliberating about it and based on their intimate knowledge of the victim. Given the links between DA and IPF, and the instrumentality of coercively controlling behaviors as well as DA, it is proposed that these offenders use DA for more than just avoiding detection. Evidence from the literature on IPV as well as DA is used to argue that offenders use DA as a vehicle for control after an IPF. This provides opportunities for offenders to control the narrative surrounding the victim's death and thus the relationship: to blame victims; to take revenge on the victims' loved ones; and to enhance their masculine status by portraying themselves in a positive, sympathetic way. It may also successfully prevent offenders from being held responsible for the murder. In this way, IPF and DA are inextricably linked and sometimes incredibly attractive to coercively controlling offenders.

The next chapter will explore how DA can best be recognized in sudden death investigations. The challenges modern detectives face in conducting death investigations and investigations in general are outlined, including the key barriers associated with uncovering concealed homicides. Opportunities for better policy and practice are proposed using case examples from international jurisdictions, where problematic cases have led to reform and reassessment of how suspiciousness is determined at sudden death scenes.

References

Anderson, K. L. (2005). Theorizing gender in intimate partner violence research. *Sex Roles, 52*(11/12), 853–865.

Anderson, K. L. (2008). Is partner violence worse in the context of control? *Journal of Marriage and Family, 70*, 1157–1168.

Anderson, K. L., & Umberson, D. (2001). Gendering violence: Masculinity and power in men's accounts of domestic violence. *Gender & Society, 15*(3), 358–380.

Bancroft, L. (2002). *Why Does He Do That? Inside the Minds of Angry and Controlling Men*. New York: G.P. Putnam's Sons.

Crossman, K. A., Hardesty, J. L., & Raffaelli, M. (2016). "He could scare me without laying a hand on me": Mothers' experiences of nonviolent coercive control during marriage and after separation. *Violence against Women, 22*, 454–473.

DeKeseredy, W., & Schwartz, M. (2009). *Dangerous Exits: Escaping Abusive Relationships in Rural America*. Piscataway, NJ: Rutgers University Press.

Dobash, R. E., & Dobash, R. P. (2015). *When men murder women*. New York: Oxford University Press.

Douglas, H., & Stark, T. (2010). *Stories from Survivors: Domestic Violence and Criminal Justice Interventions*. University of Queensland Law Research Series. http://www5.austlii.edu.au/au/journals/UQLRS/2010/6.html

Dutton, M. A., & Goodman, L. A. (2005). Coercion in intimate partner violence: Toward a new conceptualization. *Sex Roles, 52*, 743–756.

Eke, A. (2007). *Staging in cases of homicide: Offender victim and offence characteristics* (Unpublished Doctoral Thesis). York University.

Ellis, D., & DeKeseredy, W. (1997). Rethinking estrangement, interventions and intimate femicide. *Violence against Women, 3*(6), 590–609.

Ferguson, C. (2015). Staged homicides: An examination of common features of faked burglaries, suicides, accidents and car accidents. *Journal of Police and Criminal Psychology, 30*(3), 139–157, doi: 10.1007/s11896-014-9154-1

Ferguson, C. (2016) Collision or collusion? Homicides staged as car accidents. *Journal of Law and Medicine.* 24, 493–503.

Ferguson, C. & Petherick, W. (2016) Getting away with murder: An examination of detected homicides staged as suicides. *Homicide Studies, 20*(1), 3–24, doi: 10.1177/1088767914553099

Ferguson, C. & Pooley, K. (2019). Comparing solved and unsolved no-body homicides in Australia: An exploratory analysis. *Homicide Studies, 23* (4), 381–403. doi: 10.1177/10887679198523

Ferguson, C. (September, 2018). *Forensically aware offenders and homicide investigations: Challenges, opportunities and impacts.* Paper presented at Australia and New Zealand Forensic Science Society Biennial Symposium, Perth, Australia.

Ferguson C., & Sutherland, T. (2018). Murder by pushing: An exploratory analysis of homicidal falls from a height. *American Journal of Forensic Medicine and Pathology.* doi: 10.1097/PAF.0000000000000386

Ferguson, C., Doley, R., Watt, B., Lyneham, M., & Payne, J. (2015). Arson associated homicide in Australia: a 5-year follow up. *Trends and Issues in Criminology, No. 484.* Australian Institute of Criminology: Canberra.

Flacco, A. (1995). *A checklist for murder: The true story of Robert John Peernock.* New York: Diversion Books.

Graham-Kevan, N., & Archer, J. (2008). Does controlling behavior predict physical aggression and violence to partners? *Journal of Family Violence, 23*(7), 539–548.

Guzik, K. (2008). The agencies of abuse: Intimate abusers' experience of presumptive arrest and prosecution. *Law & Society Review, 42*(1), 111–144.

Hardesty, J. L., Crossman, K. A., Haselschwerdt, M. L., Raffaelli, M., Ogolsky, B. G., & Johnson, M. P. (2015). Toward a standard approach to operationalizing coercive control and classifying violence types. *Journal of Marriage and Family, 77,* 833–843.

Johnson, H., Eriksson, L., Mazerolle, P., & Wortley, R. (2019). Intimate femicide: The role of coercive control. *Feminist Criminology, 14*(1), 3–23. doi: 10.1177/55708511701574

Johnson, M. P. (2008). *A typology of domestic violence.* Lebanon, NH: Northeastern University Press.

Juodis, M., Starzomski, A., Porter, S., & Woodworth, M. (2014). A comparison of domestic and non-domestic homicides: Further evidence for distinct dynamics and heterogeneity of domestic homicide perpetrators. *Journal of Family Violence, 29,* 299–313.

Lischick, C. W. (1999). Coping and related characteristics delineating battered women's experiences in self-defined, difficult/hurtful dating relationships: A multicultural study. *Dissertation Abstracts International: Section B. Sciences and Engineering, 60*(5), 2349.

Lischick, C. W. (2009). Divorce in the context of coercive control. In E. Stark & E. Buzawa (Eds.), *Violence against women in families and relationships* (Vol. 2, pp. 191–124). Santa Barbara, CA: Praeger.

Melzer, S. A. (2002). Gender, work, and intimate violence: Men's occupational violence spillover and compensatory violence. *Journal of Marriage & Family, 64*(4), 820–832.

Monckton Smith, J. (2019). Intimate partner femicide: Using Foucauldian analysis to track an eight stage relationship progression to homicide. *Violence against Women.* doi: 10.1177%2F1077801219863876

Monckton Smith, J., Szymanska, K., & Haile, S. (2017). *Exploring the Relationship between Stalking and Homicide.* Suzy Lamplugh Trust. https://www.equallyours.org.uk/suzylamplughtrustreportexploringrelationshipstalking homicide/

Moran, J. (24 October, 1991). Man convicted of killing wife gets life term. *Los Angeles Times.*

Ornstein, P., & Rickne, J. (2013). When does intimate partner violence continue after separation? *Violence against Women, 19*, 617–633.

Peralta, R., & Tuttle, L. (2013). Male perpetrators of heterosexual-partner-violence: The role of threats to masculinity. *Journal of Men's Studies, 21*(3), 255–276. doi: 10.3149/jms.2103.255

Quinn, J. (9 July, 1991). Man goes on trial in wife's fatal beating. *Los Angeles Times.*

Stark, E. (2007). *Coercive control: How men entrap women in personal life.* New York: Oxford University Press.

Stark, E. (2009). Rethinking coercive control. *Violence against Women, 15*(12), 1509–1525. doi: 10.1177/1077801209347452

Stark, E. (2012). Looking beyond domestic violence: Policing coercive control. *Journal of Police Crisis Negotiations, 12*(2), 199–217. doi: 10.1080/15332586.2012.725016

Stark, E., & Hester, M. (2019). Coercive control: Update and review. *Violence against Women, 25*(1), 81–104. doi: 10.1177/1077801218816191

Websdale, N. S., & Johnson, B. (1997). The policing of domestic violence in rural and urban areas: The voices of battered women in Kentucky. *Policing and Society, 6*(4), 297–317. https://doi.org/10.1080/10439463.1997.9964759

Wilson, M., & Daly, M. (1992). Spousal homicide and risk estrangement. *Violence and Victims, 8*, 3–16.

Wood, J. T. (2004). Monsters and victims: Male felons' accounts of intimate partner violence. *Journal of Social and Personal Relationships, 21*(5), 555–576.

7 Challenges and opportunities in uncovering concealed homicides

This chapter outlines some of the key challenges facing police detectives who are responsible for investigating sudden deaths possibly involving DA. These challenges range from requirements in personal skill to systemic issues associated with the global push toward police transparency and accountability. To address these issues and prevent suspicious deaths from remaining concealed by the DA of offenders, police agencies and academics have made recommendations and suggested policy reform to assist detectives making decisions about suspiciousness at death scenes. Training initiatives focusing on critical thinking, communication and suspending judgment have been proposed in many jurisdictions and are canvassed in this chapter. Recommendations to increase supervision of detectives investigating sudden deaths have similarly been made as well as those to develop and improve police standard procedure in this area, especially in the form of investigative aids or checklists. Finally, reform to policy surrounding investigations into deaths that most commonly involve DA – those of women separating from controlling, abusive partners – have been advised and are discussed in this chapter. However, whether policy reform alone will address the challenges posed by DA in homicide cases is questioned.

In Mississauga, Canada, between 2009 and 2013, three members of the Harrison family died unexpectedly in the same home, in separate incidents. All three deaths were investigated by the Peel Regional Police.

Bill Harrison was discovered deceased by his wife in the bathroom of their home in April 2009, having suffered a suspected heart problem and falling to the floor. He had injuries to his forehead, nose and had a fractured sternum, all believed to be the result of his fall. There were also marks visible on his neck, perhaps attributable to a chain necklace he was wearing. Possible innocent explanations for these injuries led to his death being ruled as resulting from natural causes, and police did not investigate it as suspicious. Bill's body was cremated within days. On the day of his death, Bill's two grandchildren, whom he and his wife shared custody of, were abducted by their mother and her partner. The children were the subject of a contentious custody battle between the Harrison's and their son's ex-wife. In the hours surrounding Bill's death, the children were removed from school and taken to another province. They did not return until the arrest of their mother for parental child abduction some months later. Because Bill's death was not thought to be suspicious, links between it and the abduction of his grandchildren were not made, or even suspected.

The following year, Bill's wife Bridget Harrison was discovered deceased at the bottom of the stairs in the same house. Her body was found by one of the now-returned grandchildren when he arrived home from school. The day after Bridget's death, she was set to give evidence against her ex-daughter-in-law in the child abduction case. Forensic pathologists determined that Bridget died of neck injuries, the cause of which could not be established. The injuries appeared to be from either a fall down the stairs or strangulation, but neither could be said for certain. Bridget's death was investigated as possibly suspicious; however, foul play was eventually ruled out by police and the matter was closed.

Bill and Bridget's adult son, Caleb Harrison, died from neck compressions during a physical assault in his bedroom in August 2013, three years after his mother's death. Caleb's death first appeared to be the result of a late-night break in, and it was therefore investigated as a homicide from the outset. Upon investigating Caleb's death, the third in the same house in four years, police decided to reexamine the other unexpected deaths of Bill and Bridget. Under pressure from the remaining family members and the public, police eventually determined that both Bridget and Caleb were victims of homicides, with the offenders staging the crime scenes to appear as an accident or burglary-related death, respectively. The manner of Bill's death remains undetermined owing to the fact that the circumstances were not deemed suspicious at the time and his body was quickly cremated. For the murder of Caleb, two offenders have since been convicted: Caleb's ex-wife and her partner. The partner has also been convicted of the murder of Bridget Harrison, after confessing to both homicides. The circumstances surrounding the death of Bill Harrison remain contentious and the death is now unlikely to ever be convincingly resolved, unless new information is given by an offender.

Unfortunately, as discussed in Chapter 2, homicides being misclassified as non-suspicious deaths due to the often-simple DA behaviors of offenders are not uncommon (Ferguson & Sutherland, 2018). Examples where homicides are eventually uncovered can be found in most police jurisdictions in the western world. Perhaps more concerning, deaths and missing people classified as non-suspicious and closed but remaining controversial are also numerous. The resulting conclusion is that DA behaviors used by offenders can and do work to delay or prevent homicides from being adequately investigated and properly resolved.

In 2018, the Peel Regional Police conducted an administrative review (heretofore referred to as *the administrative review*) of all three Harrison deaths to determine how the true cause might have been detected earlier and to prevent subsequent investigative mistakes (Paolini & McKenzie,

2020). Though specific to this particular police agency, the findings of the administrative review highlight issues present in many police services – issues contributing to suspicious deaths being misclassified as non-suspicious due to offenders' DA behaviors. This chapter explores these and other personal, systemic and policy issues that hamper detectives' correctly classifying deaths when DA is involved. Following that, evidence-based policy that might combat some of these challenges and prevent DA from impacting death investigations is reviewed and best practices are proposed.

Challenges of modern detective work

Along with issues specific to death investigation, there are several broader issues with crime detection that impact on police detectives being able to recognize and adequately respond to suspicious deaths involving DA. These include criminals becoming more technologically savvy, thus crime detection must involve more technical work and expertise; detectives relying more on technology at the expense of necessary communication skills required to discover when deaths are suspicious; and evidence of diminished morale in detectives, alongside increased workloads and risk aversion in police work across the board. Each of these issues warrants a brief discussion.

Offenders becoming more tech savvy

In 2013, Westera et al. published two studies exploring how to define an effective detective and outlining skills required to develop effective detectives in the future. Researchers interviewed 30 detectives at various ranks in Australia and New Zealand. Participants were asked about the skills, abilities and personal characteristics required to be an effective detective as well as the challenges facing detectives now and into the future. One of the most frequently discussed challenges was the use of technology by offenders, and detectives' need to use technology to keep up to speed with increasingly complex investigations. Westera, Kebbell, Milne and Green (2013b) note that offenders using technology more often in their offending has changed the way that crime is detected and investigated, requiring detectives to gather evidence from surveillance, electronic intercepts and other forms of electronic communication, such as social media. According to Westera et al. (2013b, p. 2):

> the benefits of the evidential trail created by technology advances meant that gathering this type of information was now seen as a routine investigative task. Detectives were, however, concerned that they were struggling to keep up with increasingly technologically savvy criminals.

A study of homicide investigations and investigators in England and Wales finds similar results (Pike, 2018, p. 208). Worryingly, this suggests that the increasing use of technology by offenders is a concern across various crime types, including murder, and highlights the skills required of modern death investigators. Such concerns appear to have been realized in many examples of deaths involving DA such that the death becomes difficult to classify, or indeed is misclassified, as with the Harrison deaths outlined at the beginning of the chapter. In these homicides, offenders may conduct internet research or use social media to create a non-suspicious façade, while detectives may find electronic information about a suspect's whereabouts at crucial times imperative to gather quickly after discovering the death. As noted in Westera and colleagues' (2013b) work in Australia and New Zealand, the volume and scope of offending now involving the use of technology requires that detectives have the time and skill to analyze often complex, technical and voluminous data. On top of already heavy workloads, this adds a real challenge to investigators' abilities to efficiently and effectively detect many types of crimes, including suspicious deaths, and especially when offenders actively avoid detection.

Detective skills

If offenders' increasing use of technology requires investigators to develop and maintain technical skills, it is unsurprising that other important skills may fall by the wayside. Consistent with previous research (Smith & Flanagan, 2000), the most commonly cited skill or personal characteristic of effective detectives in Westera, Kebbell, Milne and Green's (2013a) first study was communication – the ability to talk to anyone, anywhere, at any time. Unfortunately, the second study by Westera et al. (2013b) reveals that this most crucial skill was perceived as being sacrificed to more technical abilities in recent years. According to Westera et al. (2013b, p. 3), "Detectives were also concerned that some detectives were relying on the abundance of electronic information when conducting investigations instead of face-to-face communication, causing this core skill to be neglected and lost". Research from England and Wales reveals similar deficits in communication skills in detectives (Brookman, Maguire, & Maguire, 2018; Pike, 2018). Pike's (2018, p. 213) research examining homicide detectives and investigations shows that "participants reported that today's detectives are not as good at speaking to people as they were historically, the loss of skills was discussed more generally and often in respect of the growing influence of science and technology". For example, investigators may be well versed in DNA collection and thus keen to use this type of evidence; however, they may lack skills in conducting neighborhood canvasses and therefore are unsuccessful at, or avoid, doing so (Pike, 2018). Brodeur and Dupont (2006) find that cases where the suspect was not swiftly identified are often problematic and difficult to solve due to deficits in detectives' communication skills and more traditional detective work not being completed at the outset. Arguably then, the loss of communication skills could prove detrimental to death investigations, especially to those which are protracted or complex, perhaps due to the use of DA by offenders.

Systemic issues affecting detective work

In the last several years, a number of studies have examined systematic issues and their impact on crime detection in various police forces, including the effect of these issues on suspicious death determination. In 2008, on behalf of the Joint Central Committee of the Police Federation of England and Wales, Michael Chatterton held 27 focus groups with detectives from the General Office Criminal Investigative Division (GO CID) who represented both countries. According to Chatterton (2008, p. vi):

> GO CID investigate serious crimes at the local Basic Command Unit (BCU) level. Their work is the hardest to categorise because they have a fluid remit but in most areas they are responsible for investigating suspicious deaths, and carrying out investigations on behalf of the coroner, amongst other serious crime.

The results of Chatterton's (2008) focus groups expose a number of worrying issues impacting on the detection of suspicious deaths and indeed, homicides. These issues include a lack of training, massive caseloads, low morale leading to difficulty retaining good detectives, low levels of experience and significant reductions in the quality of resulting investigations (Chatterton, 2008). Individuals from GO CID offices are usually the first to attend possibly suspicious deaths rather than members of specialized teams such as Major Incident or Homicide. Thus, consequences of all of these issues, most notably a lack of training and experience, can have real effects on death investigations. Both in the UK and elsewhere, it is GO CID investigators or their equivalents who are most often the police officers responsible for determining the "correct" definition of a death and how/whether each death investigation should be passed on to a specialist unit (Chatterton, 2008; Pike, 2018).

Since many western systems are set up to have general investigators (Criminal Investigative Division (CID), Criminal Investigation Branch (CIB), etc.) make initial decisions about suspiciousness at death scenes, the workload and morale of these officers are paramount to ensuring good death investigations. Chatterton's (2008) study and of others (see Brookman et al., 2018; Pike, 2018; Westera et al., 2013a, 2013b) have unfortunately found that workload is often high and morale is often low in these investigative units. For example, Chatterton's (2008) participants expressed concern for the welfare of detectives in generalist units, where extreme workloads and long hours led to mistakes invariably occurring as a result. Participants specifically noted concerns about vital evidence being lost or contaminated due to their required 24/7 response and a lack of adequate staff (Chatterton, 2008). Chatterton (2008, p. xi) notes:

> [the] everyday reality of GO CID work is represented by the resort to unprofessional coping tactics (which are a mirror image of what the organisation does at a formal level), delayed investigations which can result in discontinued cases, intelligence packages that are never actioned, and serious crimes that are not investigated.

In Australia and New Zealand, Westera et al. (2013b, p. 2) find similar concerns held by detectives:

> High stress levels and a poor work-life balance due to the serious nature of the work, a high workload, growing amounts of paperwork, working over-time, and the requirement to be on call to respond to serious crime as it happens.

This can all lead to diminishing morale, experienced detectives taking on other roles and mistakes. Both studies find that morale was further impacted by an inability to fill detective roles when staff leave, meaning that remaining personnel become even more overworked, stressed and unmotivated, making them more likely to also move on from the post (Chatterton, 2008; Westera et al., 2013b). These issues result in a loss of experience across these units in general, meaning that fewer experienced detectives are available to train and develop skills in newer detectives, further exacerbating the problem (Westera et al., 2013b).

In Australia, New Zealand, England and Wales, at least in generalist units in charge of first responding to sudden deaths, trainee detectives are not always treated as such. Due to a lack of staff and/or increasing workloads, trainees are often given caseloads despite having not completed or not even commenced their detective training (Chatterton, 2008; Pike, 2018). Indeed, in some states in Australia, investigators may go from performing general duties in uniform one day to investigating anything that comes across their desk in a generalist investigative unit (such as CIB) the next. While supervision is required for new investigators, caseloads, a lack of experienced supervisors and time pressure may impact on the quality and amount of supervision received. Trainee detectives are also often relegated to night shifts due to their lack of seniority, where they may not be accompanied by a trained and experienced detective (Chatterton, 2008).

When training is delivered, participants are not always confident in its usefulness. Traditionally, training in England and Wales was delivered through a ten-week detective training course (Pike, 2018; Tong, 2009). This generally focused on the law, but topics such as forensic issues and how to give evidence in court were also covered. In Pike's (2018) conversations with detectives, some felt that the training did not cover important elements of investigation, but instead focused on legal aspects almost exclusively. These detectives remarked that the training did not prepare them for the reality of detective work, leading to the question – how do detectives learn to investigate? The answer appears to be that they learn from others and on the job, through their own initiative and instinct. Given the complexity of investigating suspicious deaths, especially those involving DA by offenders, this lack of training and learning by osmosis alone is not ideal.

The last systemic issue impacting on detectives' ability to investigate crime in general and sudden deaths in particular is accountability. Many scholars, publishing in the area of policing and detective work, remark on the increased accountability of police to the public today (see Mulgan, 2000; Westera et al., 2013b). For example, Mulgan (2000) notes that police services have had to adapt criminal investigative processes to meet public demands for government agencies to be more transparent. Such demands lead investigators to feel that they are "being micro-managed to avoid the risk of adverse public scrutiny, which at times resulted in investigative decisions being driven by management rather than detectives" (Westera et al., 2013b, p. 3). Westera and colleagues' (2013b) research in Australia also notes detectives' concern about indirect impacts of this accountability and transparency, resulting in the public, and therefore offenders, having more knowledge of police methods of investigation. Such a concern by frontline detectives is important to the discussion of the use of DA by offenders, especially given the possible link between DA and forensic awareness (see Chapters 1, 2 and 5).

To summarize, there are several external and systemic issues that appear to be impacting on detectives' abilities to adequately investigate criminal behavior, including in possible suspicious deaths. Across several jurisdictions, the skill, experience, training and support required for good detective work appear greatly undervalued (Chatterton, 2008). Working alongside increased public knowledge of investigative strategies and offenders' increased use and availability of technology, this situation is worrisome. Despite many roadblocks that are out of their control, detectives still report a desire to conduct good investigations leading to successful prosecutions, when sufficient resources allow for this (Chatterton, 2008). This desire creates an opportunity to offer training and reform policy specific to particular tasks detectives require assistance with, such as with sudden death investigation. Such training and policy could provide simple, evidence-based rules or decision points, supporting detectives to make good judgments more efficiently, and reducing risk without overmanaging. In response to problematic cases, some police agencies have begun to take steps toward training and policy reform.

Training specific to death investigation and DA

As alluded to above, and according to Chatterton (2008, p. iii), detectives who make decisions about suspicious deaths "are simply not being fully trained". This finding was exemplified in the problematic deaths involving the Harrison family investigated by the Peel Regional Police in Canada, described at the beginning of this chapter. In the administrative review into the Harrison deaths, one of the key recommendations to prevent similar instances happening in the future involved specific death investigation training for detectives being offered and indeed required (Paolini & McKenzie, 2020). The agency already offers some death investigation training incorporated into other courses such as major crime or general investigations; however, additional training specific to death investigation was recommended for preventing mistakes in sudden death investigation.

The academic literature adds that the learning required of such training should include communication, critical thinking and investigative skills not addressed in other training as well as necessary legal elements of death investigation (Westera et al., 2013a). According to Westera et al. (2013a, p. 2), "basic communication skills – such as building rapport, explaining the process, questioning and active listening should be integral to any detective training programme". Similar training has been recommended or offered in other jurisdictions in addition to Peel. For example, after a problematic double murder that was misclassified as a murder-suicide in Queensland, Australia, the third Coroner to investigate recommended training investigators to avoid confirmation bias and to systematically assess competing investigative theories. Coroner Michael Barnes (2013, p. 122) suggested that:

> police services examine their detective training courses to assess whether they teach their officers rational criteria to equip them to choose between contending theories and to continue to gather and analyse all evidence that might be relevant until it is shown not to be. Of course, competing theories have to be abandoned as evidence disproves them, but it is essential that not be done precipitously. I commend that recommendation to the [Queensland Police Service].

The Peel Regional Police administrative review was less specific in the requirements of its recommended training; however, the sentiment appears similar to both the Queensland recommendations and those in the academic literature. The administrative review recommends that the agency develop a sudden death investigations training course as a requirement for any officer investigating sudden deaths. It was envisaged that the course would include (adapted from Paolini & McKenzie, 2020, p. 119):

1. A review of relevant directives and legislation so officers understand the law surrounding sudden death investigations, and the specific procedures required by agency policy
2. A review of case studies, lessons learned and best practices, including a detailed assessment of the Harrison deaths so that those shortcomings are recognized and avoided

3 An introduction to the use of forensic science as an investigative asset, including its scope and limitations
4 Input/participation from partner agencies such as the Coroner's Office, forensic pathology and forensic science services
5 An overview of the *Goudge Report*, which was a detailed assessment of a major failure involving forensic pathology in the years preceding the Harrison deaths (Goudge, 2008)

In terms of how the training is delivered, many academic authors note that the style of training offered is important to learning, practicing and retaining required skills (Ericsson, Krampe, & Tesch- Römer, 1993; Hattie & Timperley, 2007; Powell, Fisher, & Wright, 2005; Westera et al, 2013a). For example, training that is scenario-based, taking place across time and with gradual increases in complexity is highly recommended to develop expertise. Along with this, feedback from experts is required immediately so that mistakes can be identified and learning reinforced (Ericsson et al., 1993; Hattie & Timperley, 2007; Powell, Fisher, & Wright, 2005; Westera et al., 2013a).

One example of this type of training that the author is involved with comes from the Queensland Police Service in Australia. At this agency, basic death investigation training is given to officers new to an investigative role by the Detective Training Section during general detective training. This training prides itself on developing the behaviors, skills and knowledge required of modern investigators using adult and social learning theories. Though the content covered is broad, including areas from victim support to giving evidence and modern evidence collection techniques, practical death investigation modules are also offered. These modules are practical, immersive and scenario-based, featuring cases of various complexities that resulted in mistakes by well-meaning investigators at the time of the incident. Trainees are first given a small amount of theory about death investigation and about thinking systematically to make good decisions at death scenes. The officers are then broken into groups and asked to investigate two scenarios. The first involves basic case material and photos from a death scene, where trainee groups attempt to establish whether the death may be suspicious. Groups are asked to think analytically about the evidence to make a decision as to whether additional investigative resources (e.g., establishing a crime scene, calling for specialist unit, etc.) are required to determine suspiciousness – routine decisions in police work at this level. As the groups work through the evidence provided, expert feedback is given using probing questions and the *Socratic method*. Finally, each group is asked to present to the whole cohort of students, systematically outlining their key findings and explaining their decision-making for feedback.

The second scenario in this training involves trainee groups attending a more complex mock crime scene (this time involving a staged suicide). At the scene, groups are asked to make decisions regarding whether the death may be suspicious using a methodical assessment of the evidence available, and under time pressure. Groups are given expert feedback and asked pointed questions to assist with their decision-making. They are then required to explain their decisions to the entire cohort. Such scenario-based learning, though simple and relatively inexpensive to administer, allows trainees to consider the merits of evidence in real cases, to understand their own limitations in knowledge and experience, to practice thinking critically by suspending judgment under realistic conditions and to learn from the mistakes of colleagues who came before them. Training like this is highly regarded by trainees, providing them with an opportunity to practice making suspicious death determinations in a low risk environment and providing reassurance around arguing to engage additional resources.

Alongside training programs such as this, several agencies have also developed policy to help overcome barriers to efficient and effective suspicious death investigations. These policies commonly establish rules for triaging cases to more senior detectives, require more oversight for certain types of deaths or establish specific procedures for investigators making determinations of suspiciousness.

Policy reform to overcome challenges

Together with training, common policy reform recommendations coming out of reviews of problematic suspicious death investigations generally surround increased supervision or oversight for detectives investigating deaths, additions to standard procedure in the form of investigative aids for establishing suspiciousness and less commonly, broader level changes surrounding how deaths of women are investigated.

Supervision

One broad policy recommendation that has been made in a number of regions in recent years surrounds establishing more effective procedures for how and when more experienced detectives supervise potentially suspicious death investigations. For example, in the problematic double murder in Queensland, Australia, described earlier in this chapter, Coroner Barnes noted that a key issue was lack of supervision. In this case, the absence of supervision led to the double murder remaining misclassified as a murder-suicide for more than two decades. Coroner Barnes states (Barnes, 2013, p. 15):

> [Senior detectives reviewing the case some years after the deaths] noted that the more senior police who should have been supervising [the detective in charge], failed to recognise or respond to the complexity of the crime scene. [Reviewing detectives] noted that expert assistance was available through the Homicide Squad in Brisbane but was not sought due to the cost involved and that supervising police should have

> recognised at an early stage that [the detective in charge], the principal investigator, was not experienced in the investigation of homicide, particularly complex homicides such as this case. [The detective in charge] was given little assistance and guidance in carrying out the investigation. [Senior detectives conducting a review] were not critical of the late [detective in charge] whom they considered to be a regional police officer doing his best but who was out of his depth. Rather, they pointed out that [the detective's] superiors should have seen the need for expert assistance from the Homicide Squad at an early stage.

Unfortunately, more specialized supervision was not given, resulting in more than 20 years of mistakes, controversies and reinvestigation in this problematic case. In response to these problems, Coroner Barnes recommended that the responsible policing agency implement a policy where briefs of evidence prepared for the coroner by police detectives are carefully considered by either a more experienced senior officer or a detective working in the specialized Coronial Support Unit (Barnes, 2013). This would ensure that the available evidence is both adequate and satisfactory for the conclusions drawn before it is forwarded to the Coroner. Since the deaths but prior to Barnes' recommendations, the Queensland Police Service instituted a policy similar to this recommendation, requiring that District Officers review briefs of evidence surrounding possible suspicious deaths. This updated Queensland policy is a much more stringent criterion than was required at the time the deaths were misclassified in 1991 (Barnes, 2013).

More recently, the administrative review of the Harrison deaths in Peel recommended changes to policy that would require more supervision and approvals for closing sudden death investigations at the police rather than coronial level (Peel Review, 2020). In such cases, it was recommended that relevant CIB detective sergeants be required to review the investigation and approve its closure before this occurs. In so doing, detective sergeants may require that investigating officers gather additional information or continue the investigation. For when suspicious or sudden death investigations cannot reach a result, it was recommended that Peel Regional Police require that a detective trained in homicide investigation conduct a peer review of the file prior to the investigation being closed. Such a recommendation ensures that equivocal cases are not closed until all lines of inquiry have been exhausted. Finally, the administrative review also recommended that all sudden death investigations be reviewed by an assigned detective sergeant from the homicide unit on a monthly basis (Paolini & McKenzie, 2020). The administrative review noted that this "will add another level of oversight that will ensure that all cases of sudden death are adequately investigated" (2020, p. 122).

While these are positive developments in policy, hopefully leading to more thorough and complete investigations, these initiatives are less helpful for preventing deaths being misclassified in the short term – at the death scene and in the days and hours after discovery. By the time a brief of evidence is completed or a case is ready to be closed and is thus reviewed by senior officers, scenes are likely to have been released, bodies cremated or interred and evidence possibly lost. Other agencies have recommended or implemented additional policy in the hopes of preventing problematic decision-making earlier in an investigation. These policies generally involve providing evidence-based investigative aids or checklists to be used to gather potential evidence of suspiciousness in the very earliest assessment of a sudden death – usually by general detectives or uniformed police attending as first responders.

Investigative aids

As one example, along with enhanced supervision, the Peel Regional Police administrative review (2020) recommended the development of an investigative aid (checklist) for sudden death investigations. It was envisaged that the checklist would provide a list of investigative considerations, including scene and circumstantial factors that must be addressed. For example, investigating officers would be responsible for considering and documenting factors such as (Paolini & McKenzie, 2020, p. 120):

- Presence of blood at the scene
- Evidence of injury to the deceased or reporting party
- Age and previous health of the deceased
- Past history of domestic violence
- Pending court cases or separation, divorce proceedings, child custody, civil actions, judicial hearings

According to the administrative review, such a checklist would "ensure that all required notifications and follow ups are done and the checklist must be signed off by CIB Detective Sergeant" (Paolini & McKenzie, 2020, p. 120).

Other agencies have gone further and have been more specific in investigative aids for establishing the suspiciousness of a death above and beyond the normal inquiries required (e.g., of basic death investigation inquiries, see *National Institute of Justice Technical Update* by Holder, Robinson, & Laub, 2011). For instance, the author assisted the Edmonton Police Service in Canada to implement evidence-based decision points that would assist investigators with resource allocation and escalation of incidents to specialist teams. The policy being implemented first includes a requirement that officers conduct no less than two interviews to establish decedent history. These could include interviews with the reporting party and the next of kin, or next of kin and an additional family member or close contact. This requirement was established so that the history given for the decedent could be compared across those close to them. The policy then provides a checklist of investigative questions above the normal inquiries required in a sudden death investigation and instructions for answering them. Answering yes to any of the questions indicates that additional investigative steps are required before the death may be ruled non-suspicious. In summary form, this checklist includes the following considerations:

1. *Is this an apparent suicide, falling death* (Ferguson & Sutherland, 2018) *or overdose*? If so, answer yes. If this cannot be determined at the scene, answer yes.
2. *Was the scene unsecured on discovery (e.g., decedent found inside an unlocked home)*? Answer yes if it is probable that others besides the decedent and reporter had access to the scene between the death and discovery, or if this cannot be verified.
3. *Does the decedent have a history of domestic violence victimization, reported or unreported to police*? Answer yes if history collected from witnesses, close associates and police files indicates the decedent has ever been the victim of domestic violence, stalking, coercion and/or controlling behavior in an intimate relationship.
4. *Does the history of the next of kin, closest associates or family include a criminal history of deception, violence, arson* (Schlesinger, Gardenier, Jarvis, & Sheehan-Cook, 2012) *or do they have a known history of making insurance claims*? To answer this question, it is necessary to determine who the closest people are in the decedent's life and inquire as to whether they have charges, convictions or are under investigation for behaviors related to fraud, obstruction of police/justice, perjury, identity theft, forgery, personation, violence, arson, parental abduction and so on. It should also be considered whether there is a history of insurance claims that may be indicative of undiscovered fraudulent acts, deception or manipulation.
5. *Are there any provable lies provided by close associates, reporter or next of kin*? Comparing the statements received: Do any of the facts conflict? If so, answer yes.
6. *Has the body position changed between death and investigation (including for CPR, first aid, checking vital signs) and/or are there unexplained blood stains at the scene*? This can be assessed by doing a basic visual assessment of lividity, rigor mortis, evidence of movement through blood stains and the surrounding environment in comparison to the suspected narrative surrounding the death. Answer yes if there is any evidence that the decedent's body has been moved, even if under instruction. Investigators should also consider whether first aid was administered or vital signs checked under instruction from emergency services. This may be done through an assessment of transfer evidence on to the reporting party.
7. *Is any individual close to the decedent advocating for further investigation*? If anyone close to the decedent is skeptical about the apparent manner of death, answer yes.

8 *Did the decedent's pattern of behavior appear to change leading to the death*? For example, does the scene appear as a suicide despite family reporting the decedent was in good spirits? Did the decedent purchase a firearm despite reports that they were afraid of guns? Consider if the decedent's behavior leading to the death was characteristic of them. Answer yes if behavior patterns changed shortly before the death.
9 *Did the decedent present a financial liability or opportunity for someone else*? Answer yes if the decedent was a financial barrier or opportunity to any person, and if that barrier was evidenced in the history by conflict between the relevant parties. For example, lawsuits, outstanding custody disputes, impending separation or divorce, domestic arguments over money, significant debts, business disputes, the decedent's beneficiaries and the availability of life insurance policies should all be investigated. Answer yes if the decedent presents a financial opportunity or liability to someone else.
10 *Does the attending investigator express suspicion regarding the death*? This is a consideration for suspicion regarding the manner of death that may be difficult to articulate. Answer yes if investigators attending the scene have persistent suspicion despite the inquiries above.

The Edmonton Police Service and the author proposed incorporating the checklist above into death investigation policy because the checklist provides an efficient and easy-to-use series of decision points designed to assist investigators with assessing death scenes in a systematic fashion. Answering yes to any of the ten questions contained in the checklist is not to suggest that the death should necessarily be deemed suspicious. Instead, a "yes" simply indicates to investigators that they should suspend judgment until further inquiries are carried out or specialist assistance is received. When borne out of the literature on DA, CSS and concealed homicides reviewed throughout this book, policies implementing checklists such as this are designed to engage required resources as early as possible to prevent suspicious deaths from being misclassified. After the initial assessment of a death scene, when DA, CSS or homicide concealment is suspected, more detailed evidence-based investigative aids can be utilized to uncover additional lines of inquiry. For examples of these aids, see *Detecting Staged Crime Scenes: An Empirically Derived 'How-to'* (Ferguson, 2015).

Broader policy reform

In further efforts to prevent suspicious deaths from being misclassified, other academics and police agencies have suggested or implemented policy changes that are much broader than enhancing supervision or providing investigative aids. For example, in 2019, Bitton and Dayan explored concealed femicide cases in Israel. Similar to the problematic Harrison family deaths in Canada, this study came about after an offender, Shimon Cooper, was convicted of killing two wives in separate incidents in 1994 and 2009.

Both of these murders were originally resolved as suicides by virtue of CSS perpetrated by Cooper. In both of these cases, investigators did not suspend judgment. They clung to the suicide theory as indicated by the (staged) evidence at the death scene and did not take on board or further investigate evidence that tended to refute the suicide theory. Cooper was eventually convicted of both murders in 2014, 20 years and five years after the deaths, but only after intense media pressure forced police to reinvestigate. Cooper is also suspected of killing his mother, though her death remains under investigation (Zieger, 2013). Through these cases, several concerning trends in the investigation of women's deaths in Israel were revealed – most associated with the lack of a common law coronial system. To combat these issues, Bitton and Dayan (2019, pp. 1066–1067) made several policy recommendations. Some of these recommendations are specific to deaths of women, but all are relevant to other jurisdictions as the authors echo both the academic and industry literature on suspicious death investigation discussed earlier in this chapter. Each of these recommendations and the supporting literature from other countries and context warrant a brief discussion:

1 A suspicious death classification should automatically occur in a death that is unforeseen by the decedent's personal physician (Bitton & Dayan, 2019). In Bill Harrison's case, such a policy might have forced a more detailed examination of his supposed natural death from a cardiac arrest. In the Cooper deaths, both women's supposed suicides were completely unforeseen by their doctors, despite Cooper reporting depression in both women. In the similar double murder case in Queensland, Australia, the coroner admonished police for failing to take into consideration the total absence of evidence that one decedent and the supposed perpetrator of the murder-suicide involving her best friend was suicidal. In that case, Coroner Barnes (discussed above) recommended policy changes to prevent police from jumping to conclusions based on how a death scene presents (Barnes, 2013). The coroner noted (Barnes, 2013, p. 122):

> if investigators too quickly fix on or commit to a theory explaining a crime [or death] they risk failing to see evidence that may disprove it and are liable to subconsciously distort evidence they do find to make it fit into the framework of their favoured theory.

A policy requiring a suspicious death investigation to consider the professional judgment of the decedent's physician rather than solely based on the police's view of a possibly staged death scene may go some way to prevent such confirmation biases and stop concealed homicides remaining undetected.

2 In cases of suspected suicide, a full internal autopsy should be mandatory and should be conducted under the premise of a suspicious death (Bitton & Dayan, 2019). This would require forensic pathologists to actively search for evidence that is unsupportive of suicide. The results of

the autopsy should be communicated to investigating police in a timely fashion and give particular focus to whether medical findings comport with the narrative of the supposed suicide account given by next of kin or extrapolated from evidence at the death scene (Bitton & Dayan, 2019). Similar to the Cooper homicides, the administrative review conducted after the Harrison deaths in Canada uncovered major issues with communication between police and forensic medical staff, even when autopsies were conducted. Issues in both cases include autopsies being conducted under the auspices of a probable non-suspicious death, and the significance of medical findings that contradict the death scene presentation remaining unrecognized by either police or medical staff. Indeed, the Peel administrative review (Paolini & McKenzie, 2020, p. 121) recommended a similar policy change to Bitton and Dayan (2019), stating that directives to investigators should be amended to include a statement similar to one in a nearby jurisdiction. The example directive states:

> notwithstanding the coroner's official designation of death, there is nothing precluding police from continuing their investigation where there is some residual suspicion of foul play. If further investigation raises new issues, further communication should take place between the police and the coroner.

The same may also be true in the other direction, where medical staff should be required to complete more thorough investigations despite police theories of suspicious or non-suspiciousness.

The next four recommendations provided by Bitton and Dayan (2019, pp. 1066–1067) are specific to the deaths of women, and therefore they are discussed collectively with reference to literature explored previously in this book. The four recommendations are:

3 All deaths of women should require explicit investigation of her intimate relationship (Bitton & Dayan, 2019). Specifically, evidence surrounding whether the decedent or her partner wished to or were in the process of separating should be sought out as a matter of policy. If found, this evidence should render the death suspicious.

4 All deaths of women should require explicit investigation of whether her intimate partner has ever perpetrated violence against previous partners, family members, relatives or acquaintances as well as the decedent herself (Bitton & Dayan, 2019). If found, this evidence should render the death suspicious.

5 All deaths of women found in their home should be deemed suspicious deaths and investigated as such (Bitton & Dayan, 2019).

6 All deaths of women discovered by their current or previous intimate partner should be deemed suspicious deaths and investigated as such (Bitton & Dayan, 2019).

As discussed in Chapter 6 on DA and coercive control, the literature on women's risk of homicide is clear in showing that risk goes up significantly during separation from an abusive intimate partner, whether they take steps to facilitate the separation or only discuss or threaten it (Johnson, Eriksson, Mazerolle, & Wortley, 2019; Juodis et al., 2014 Monckton Smith, 2019). These cases commonly involve CSS or concealment through DA. Notably, cases that are at a high risk of homicide do not require evidence of physical violence in the relationship (Lischick, 1999, 2009; Stark & Hester, 2019). Cases involving more subtle coercive control may be equally or more risky (Stark & Hester, 2019), meaning that police investigating deaths of women may have to look beyond overt evidence of assaults or violence to establish a history of abuse. Seeking out evidence from past partners is useful for establishing how a decedent's intimate partner behaves in a relationship when the decedent herself cannot give evidence. As indicated in the last chapter, the link between coercive control and attempts to conceal an IPF through DA are strong. Concealment often involves the offender killing the victim in her own home and reporting discovering the scene to police (Eke, 2007; Monckton Smith, 2019). Therefore, policy changes such as the above recommended by Bitton and Dayan (2019) are well supported in the academic literature.

Should policy reform be the solitary focus?

Before concluding this discussion on preventing the impacts of offender DA on death investigations, one word of caution is required. Much time has been devoted to discussing policy on various levels in this chapter, including a modest amount of international consensus on the necessity of policy reform. However, it should also be noted that there is some controversy over whether changes to policy are useful to frontline police detectives, especially when changes come in the form of increasingly prescriptive procedures for investigations of various types. This issue was alluded to in the section on challenges resulting from increased accountability in investigations and the required transparency of police procedure. The question remains – does policy change enhance investigations or hinder good investigators? Burrows et al. (2005) comment on discretionary models of investigation versus procedural models, noting that the former requires individual professional commitment from detectives, and the latter very specific procedures to be followed. Unfortunately, though more and more agencies move toward procedural models, whether these are more efficient and effective than discretionary models has not been convincingly established. Chatterton (2008, p. xiii) comments:

> The reliance on individual professional commitment is most immediately apparent in the ideal type 'discretionary' model where there is 'maximum officer ownership of cases' and maximum professional discretion at all stages'. 'Knowledgeable, professional officers capable of

> exercising good individual judgement' and operating with 'strong individual 'professional ethics' are listed as requirements. The 'procedural' model reduces the element of individual discretion by carefully delineating each stage in the investigative process and by specifying, based on best practice, what needs to be done at each stage.

The danger of such a procedural model is that some officers – perhaps burdened by the issues outlined earlier such as a lack of training and experience, long hours, increasing paperwork and so on – may blindly follow procedure without deliberating too long on information or inquiries outside of the required process. In this way, officers may be encouraged to follow the book too closely, or as noted by Burrows et al. (2005, pp. 132–133), "the individuals involved may focus on the details of the prescribed activity at the expense of attempting to achieve its purpose". Despite the necessity of policy change in this area and the usefulness of investigative aids for thinking critically and systematically, a strictly procedural model is not being advocated here. Instead, recommending evidence-based policy that creates opportunities for good investigators will create an environment for thorough suspicious death investigations. As noted by Westera and colleagues (2013a, 2013b), this means that detectives need to be trained to work within the parameters of the law, they need to understand what best practice is and how to effectively use it and they also have to be able to make decisions, communicate, work well in a team and diligently follow the evidence. As per Pike (2018, p. 213), "in both models the quality of performance depends on skill, motivation and professional pride" – qualities that should not be overshadowed by a slavish commitment to policy and procedure. Therefore, preventing misclassification of suspicious deaths requires not only good training and policy reform in this area, but also acknowledgment of the complexity of some suspicious death cases, the lack of control many investigators have over how resources are allocated to investigations and the pressures associated with a high level of scrutiny often found in this work.

Conclusion

This chapter has discussed some of the key challenges facing detectives who are responsible for investigating sudden deaths. These challenges run the gamut from requirements in personal skill to systemic issues associated with the global push toward police transparency and accountability to the public. Challenges such as these are exacerbated by offenders becoming increasingly technologically savvy and by police procedure being more widely known to the public, including to offenders who are motivated to evade those procedures. To combat these issues and prevent suspicious deaths from remaining concealed, police agencies and academics alike have recommended increased training for detectives making decisions about suspiciousness at death scenes. Such training should focus on critical thinking, communication and suspending judgment. Recommendations have also been made to increase supervision of detectives investigating sudden deaths; to develop and improve procedure in this area, especially in the form of investigative aids; and to reform policy more broadly surrounding investigations into deaths that commonly involve DA – those of women separating from controlling, abusive partners. However, along with such policy reform, the complexity of these investigations should also be acknowledged, and the necessity for supporting detectives to make good but sometimes expensive decisions, appreciated. If a balance can be struck between empowering good personnel and establishing good policy, it is possible to detect many more concealed homicides early on. Doing so would prevent myriad problems for police agencies and coroners, but more importantly would prevent families from having to fight for better investigations into their loved one's sudden deaths and uncover offenders in the timeliest possible fashion.

References

Barnes, M. (2013). Inquest into the deaths of Julie-Anne Leahy and Vicki Arnold. Officer of the State Coroner Findings of Inquest. COR91/1768. https://www.justice.qld.gov.au/__data/assets/pdf_file/0020/454304/qgr-leahy-j-arnold-v-20160125.pdf

Bitton, Y., & Dayan H. (2019). 'The perfect murder': An exploratory study of staged murder scenes and concealed femicide. *British Journal of Criminology, 59*, 1054–1079. doi: 10.1093/bjc/azz015

Brodeur, J.-P., & Dupont, B. (2006). Knowledge workers or "knowledge" workers? *Policing and Society, 16*(1), 7–26.

Brookman, F., Maguire, E. R., & Maguire, M. (2018). What factors influence whether homicide cases are solved? Qualitative evidence from Great Britain and the USA. *Homicide Studies, 23*(2), 145–174. doi: 10.1177/1088767918793678

Burrows, J., Hopkins, M., Hubbard, R., Robinson, A., Speed M., & Tilley, N. (2005). *Understanding the attrition process in volume crime investigations. Home office research study 295.* London: Home Office.

Chatterton, M. (2008). *Losing the detectives: Views from the frontline.* Surbiton: Police Federation of England and Wales. Available at: http://www.wm- ireland.com/polfed/detectives.pdf

Eke, A. (2007). *Staging in cases of homicide: Offender victim and offence characteristics* (Unpublished Doctoral Thesis). York University

Ericsson, K., Krampe, R., & Tesch-Römer, C. (1993). The role of deliberate practice in the acquisition of expert performance. *Psychological Review, 100*(3), 363–406.

Ferguson, C. (2015). Detecting staged crime scenes: An empirically derived how-to. In W. A. Petherick (Ed.), *Applied crime analysis: A social science approach to understanding crime, criminals, and victims* (pp. 80–100). Boston, MA: Anderson Publishing.

Ferguson, C., & Sutherland, T. (2018). Murder by pushing: An exploratory analysis of homicidal falls from a height. *American Journal of Forensic Medicine and Pathology, 38*(3), 192–200. doi: 10.1097/PAF.0000000000000386

Goudge, S. (2008). Inquiry into pediatric forensic pathology in Ontario. http:/// www.goudgeinquiry.ca

Hattie, J., & Timperley, H. (2007). The power of feedback. *Review of Educational Research, 77*(1), 81–112.

Holder, E., Robinson, L., & Laub, J. (2011). *Death investigation: A guide for the scene investigator.* Washington, DC: US Department of Justice.

Johnson, H., Eriksson, L., Mazerolle, P., & Wortley, R. (2019). Intimate femicide: The role of coercive control. *Feminist Criminology, 14*(1), 3–23. doi: 10.1177/55708511701574

Juodis, M., Starzomski, A., Porter, S., & Woodworth, M. (2014). A comparison of domestic and non-domestic homicides: Further evidence for distinct dynamics and heterogeneity of domestic homicide perpetrators. *Journal of Family Violence, 29*, 299–313.

Lischick, C. W. (1999). Coping and related characteristics delineating battered women's experiences in self-defined, difficult/hurtful dating relationships: A multicultural study. *Dissertation Abstracts International: Section B. Sciences and Engineering, 60*(5), 2349.

Lischick, C. W. (2009). Divorce in the context of coercive control. In E. Stark & E. Buzawa (Eds.), *Violence against women in families and relationships* (Vol. 2, pp. 191–124). Santa Barbara, CA: Praeger.

Monckton Smith, J. (2019). Intimate partner femicide: Using Foucauldian analysis to track an eight stage relationship progression to homicide. *Violence against Women, 26*(11), 1267–1285. https://doi.org/10.1177%2F1077801219863876

Mulgan, R. (2000). 'Accountability': An ever-expanding concept? *Public Administration, 78*(3), 555–573.

Paolini, J., & McKenzie, M. (2020). Administrative review – Harrison homicides. *Peel Regional Police.* https://www.peelpolice.ca/modules/news/index.aspx?newsId=90f48281-7b3d-4490-9fab-c9829195a89e

Pike, S. (2018). *A critical exploration of changes to the investigation of homicide in England and Wales from the 1980s to the present day* (Unpublished doctoral thesis). University of South Wales.

Powell, M., Fisher, R., & Wright, R. (2005). Investigative interviewing. In N. Brewer & K. Williams (Eds.), *Psychology and law: An empirical perspective.* New York: Guilford.

Schlesinger, L., Gardenier, A., Jarvis, J., & Sheehan-Cook, J. (2012). Crime scene staging in homicide. *Journal of Police and Criminal Psychology, 29*, 44–51. doi: 10.1007/s11896-012-9114-6

Smith, N., & Flanagan, C. (2000). *The effective detective: Identifying the skills of an effective SIO.* London: Home Office

Stark, E., & Hester, M. (2019). Coercive control: Update and review. *Violence against Women, 25*(1), 81–104. doi: 10.1177/1077801218816191

Tong, S. (2009). Professionalising investigations. In S. Tong, R. Bryant, & M. Horvath (Eds.), *Understanding criminal investigation* (pp. 197–216). Chichester: Wiley-Blackwell.

Westera, N., Kebbell, M., Milne, R., & Green, T. (2013a). Defining the effective detective. Briefing Paper, Issue 20. Centre of Excellence in Policing and Security.

Westera, N., Kebbell, M., Milne, R., & Green, T. (2013b). Developing the effective detective of the future. Briefing Paper, Issue 21. Centre of Excellence in Policing and Security.

Zieger, A. (2013, 19 March). "Accused wife-killer now charged with murder of first wife too". *The Times of Israel.* https://www.timesofisrael.com/accused-wife-killer-now-charged-with-murder-of-first-spouse-too/#gs.fsw83p

Index

Note: **Bold** page numbers refer to tables and *italic* page numbers refer to figures.